Praise for *My Boss is a Moron*

'Annoyingly funny, phenomenally helpful'
Chris Donnelly, entrepreneur and author

'A wake-up call for anyone stuck in a toxic job'
**Simon Squibb, entrepreneur and
author of *What's Your Dream?***

'The perfect book for anyone who is currently
struggling with their job or manager'
Eric Partaker, entrepreneur and author

'*My Boss is a Moron* delivers a hilarious yet brutally honest
glimpse into the maddening world of office politics. With sharp
prose and satire, it captures the absurdity of working under
incompetent leadership. Ben's analysis provides readers with the
tools to tackle bad managers and help workers navigate their way
to a better working life'
**Lord Mark Price, House of Lords and author of
*Happy Economics***

This book is dedicated to my amazing wife Ellen and to anyone who is struggling with their job. I hope this book makes things that little bit easier and the burden feels that little bit lighter as a result of reading it.

MY BOSS IS
A MORON

MY BOSS IS
A MORON

STRATEGIES TO MANAGE UP AND
THRIVE IN ANY WORKPLACE

BEN ASKINS

EBURY EDGE

UK | USA | Canada | Ireland | Australia
India | New Zealand | South Africa

Ebury Edge is part of the Penguin Random House group of companies
whose addresses can be found at global.penguinrandomhouse.com

Penguin Random House UK
One Embassy Gardens, 8 Viaduct Gardens, London SW11 7BW

penguin.co.uk
global.penguinrandomhouse.com

Penguin
Random House
UK

First published by Ebury Edge in 2025

Typeset in 11.69/18.78pt Warnock pro by Six Red Marbles UK, Thetford, Norfolk
Printed and bound in India by Manipal Technologies Limited

The authorised representative in the EEA is Penguin Random House Ireland,
Morrison Chambers, 32 Nassau Street, Dublin D02 YH68

A CIP catalogue record for this book is available from the British Library

ISBN 9781529146905

Contents

■ ■ ■

Introduction

...

If you are thinking about writing a book, I have a few observations that might help.

The first is that it is a lot harder than you might think. This may not be as much of a surprise to you as it was to me. I swaggered into the process. I couldn't have been more confident. A whole year to write about a topic I release daily videos about? Absolute breeze.

I was so cocky I even tried to shorten the deadline my ever-patient editor originally gave me before sheepishly returning, hat in hand, to ask for my original schedule back.

The second observation is that a combination of WhatsApp and spellcheck has completely ruined my understanding of how grammar works. Full stops and commas were fine, but I still have absolutely no idea when I am meant to use a semi-colon and developed an unhelpful tendency to throw one in every now and again just to make a paragraph feel fancier.

The final observation I would make is that when you start writing, despite having every intention of trying to sound natural and easy to understand, you start reaching for words or phrases that you have never actually used in your adult life and only have a vague idea of what they mean. This is compounded by the fact that, because the writing process takes over a year, you slightly forget what you have written in earlier chapters.

It was this perfect storm that led to my first draft containing the phrase 'pièce de résistance' on no less than eight separate occasions despite having not once ever used those words in any other context.

This book has been one of the hardest challenges I have ever set out to accomplish. Not because I didn't know what I wanted to write, but because this is such an enormous topic – and one that I have immersed myself in so thoroughly over the last couple of years – that trying to mention everything I wanted to include without requiring a whole trilogy of *Lord of the Rings* proportions was looking nearly impossible. But it was becoming increasingly obvious to me how important this topic was to address.

The world has never been less engaged with work. With post-Covid productivity numbers trending ever lower and 24 per cent of people feeling like they are working for their worst boss ever, I don't think the word 'crisis' is an exaggeration. This is made worse by the fact that for everyone dealt the hand of a bad boss is often offered only two pieces of advice: 'suck it up and get on with it', which, if you are part of a younger generation, might be allied with the added bonus of a story that starts with 'back in my day . . .', or 'go and work for yourself then'. Now, I will always encourage people to go down the entrepreneurial route if that is what they want to do, but it is unrealistic to just expect everyone to have the resources or appetite to strike out on their own. Beyond just quitting and throwing in the towel, this book is all about the third way: how to make the best of a bad situation. This book will teach you how to manage a terrible boss and present you with tactics to mitigate your circumstances and allow you to give yourself the best possible chance of success.

It is worth spending a little time talking about why I felt like I was the right person for the job.

I have been an entrepreneur now for over ten years. I built my first business, a digital marketing agency, over nine years, opening offices in both London and New York. I sold the business at the end of 2021. Since then, I have gone on to found two new businesses: a green technology company called Gaia, and my content business called Benchmark.

In short, I have been hiring, firing, managing and leading people for over a decade. In that time, I have made every possible mistake you could imagine. Much of the contents of this book is based on things I did badly as well as the bits I managed to get right. I still cringe at some of those memories.

The first time I fired someone, I did it so badly and beat around the bush so much, she didn't realise she was being fired – I had to book a second meeting to make it clear. One of the reasons I talk about the importance of management training is because of how much I know I needed it early on in my career.

But that's not why I have written this book. The reason I feel I have the knowledge and insight to put digital pen to paper is that I have had the privilege of receiving over 200,000 boss stories from my followers over the past couple of years through my social media channels. These stories come from every possible country, sector and demographic. They range from the completely ridiculous, to the everyday frustration. A lot of these stories I have shared on my channel, others I will share in this book, but the sheer scale of the data has allowed me to weave together a narrative that explains where we get it wrong, why so many bosses are making these mistakes, and what the potential solutions are when you feel you are badly managed.

There are four outcomes I wanted to achieve by writing *My Boss Is a Moron.*

The first is to let you know that you are not alone. Having a terrible boss can be one of the most isolating feelings in the world. Having no one to turn to at work can feel nothing short of devastating and can make it really challenging to even get out of bed to face the day. Having a bad boss is something everyone will experience at some point in their careers.

The second outcome is to help. And I mean really help. Not just to give you a sympathetic ear but to provide genuine advice and a blueprint for what you can do. We will cover the tips and tricks you can use to manage up and handle a bad boss, but we will also break down the situations you can improve and those where you should be thinking about moving on to a new job. One of the most heartbreaking discoveries I have made since starting my social media channels is not the people who have had terrible bosses, but the ones who have had terrible bosses and didn't even realise it.

The third outcome is to provide advice on how to run a

successful team or company. Very few people set out to be a bad boss or awful manager. Of course they don't, that would be socio-pathic. Instead, all these issues come from three main areas: a lack of awareness, a lack of communication and a lack of training.

Even the most selfish managers will recognise that a motivated, engaged and incentivised team will always outperform a team that is falling apart and quitting in droves. The commercial upside is clear for all to see. This is one of those rare moments in life where we are looking at a genuine win-win scenario where managers can do the right thing with their team that also directly benefits them.

The final outcome is to provide some light entertainment and to remind you all that work can be fun. That is not to undermine some of the truly terrible experiences that people go through, but I think one of the reasons that management and the principles of it are so underutilised at companies is because a lot of the subject matter is dull. One of the first things I said to my editor was that I would never write a stuffy manual full of long lists of the dos and don'ts of management. It just isn't my style. Learning is only pos-sible through enjoyment. A huge priority of mine was to write a book that people could read, learn from and have fun with.

I was once asked what I thought the best trait in a manager was, and I surprised everyone by saying I thought 'self-deprecation' was such an underrated quality. A boss who can take a joke is not only confident enough in their own position to laugh at themselves, but they are also much more likely not to sweat the small stuff.

So much conflict, stress and arguments are based on the small-est and tiniest of issues but, because some people are incapable of processing or handling them, they ruin the working lives of other people over it. 'Will this be important in six months' time?' is a useful barometer for what matters, and so few conflicts at work pass that test.

This book might not be what you expect. There will be some questionable metaphors, some undeniably cheesy humour, and some ridiculous stories. But the pièce de résistance of this book is that little bit of extra help to handle the absolute cretin the gods of business have bestowed upon you and your career.

1

JOB DESCRIPTIONS

Boss: *Alright mate, if you get some spare time today I need you to head downstairs and have a bit of a tidy up. We need to make space for some new shelving units.*

Employee: *Hey, I don't mind doing that but can we have a chat when you get back? I don't mind helping out but you hired me as a graphic designer and I'm getting pulled into a lot of these odd jobs.*

Boss: *I told you to expect some duties outside of the job spec mate. What did you expect?*

Employee: *I know, but I thought you meant sitting in on meetings, or making slide decks or something, not building IKEA furniture and tidying up the storage room.*

'What do you do for work?' should not be a difficult question to answer.

'How big is the universe?' Now that is a tricky one. 'How many people are there in the world called Brian?' Almost impossible. But asking what your job is? That doesn't sound like it should be anything but simple. As straightforward as telling someone your name or age.

Unfortunately, the gem that is modern working life has made

job descriptions a worthy entry into the 'it isn't that hard but some-how we make it so much trickier than it needs to be' category.

If someone asks what you do, you rarely have the time to read out a list of various duties and, if we are being honest with our-selves, it's not something you have any interest in doing either. The whole attitude of 'I deal with enough work at *actual* work, the last thing I want is to be chatting shop when I am not being paid to do so' is never more prevalent than in forced social interaction.

A job title solves both those problems. It doesn't tell you everything, but it gives you the gist, which, in the majority of con-versations, is more than enough.

If your interlocutor is someone who requires a little more information because they are genuinely interested or, more likely, you're in a social situation neither of you can escape and are politely feigning enthusiasm, there is another layer below that of job title. This is called a job description. Broadly speaking, a list of duties and job requirements that you actually do during work hours and is often used as the basis for hiring you in the first place.

Again, very, very simple.

And yet, for something so easy, we sure do seem to mess up in spectacular ways. I am bombarded on social media with stories of people disagreeing with either the company they are working for, or a business they are in the process of joining, about what it is exactly that they should be doing with their day. These range from minor squabbles to genuine contract disputes.

A good example of this latter category was the woman who messaged me telling me about her husband who applied for a job as a gardener. Halfway through the interview they informed him that he may need to take on some of the lifeguarding duties at the pool. Just to be clear, we are not talking maintenance or cleaning duties, we are talking about being an actual lifeguard. When he pointed out that he wasn't qualified to do this, their response was 'all you have to do is to watch people swim'.

Needless to say he didn't take the job, which was a shame because it meant I never did find out if this company found the pruning Aquaman they were looking for.

I have hired a lot of people throughout my career, and I have spent a great deal of time talking to people who have had issues with this side of running a business and it all seems to come down to companies and business leaders genuinely not understanding why having a proper job title attached to a job description that, firstly, makes sense and, secondly, can be accurately referred to is crucial to having a satisfied team which, in turn, leads to a more successful and profitable business.

This last point is especially relevant because if you ask any CEO in the world right now, 'Would you like your team to be more motivated and working harder?', they are never going to say no. Yet, too often these basic principles of running a successful company are viewed with the same disdain that people usually reserve for cat owners who take their pets for a walk.

Of course, we are not helping ourselves as we have a raft of job titles that are either too broad or, in some circumstances, don't actually mean anything. I have been in business for 12 years and I still have no idea what a business analyst does. It seems to be one of those essential roles that covers nearly every sector and industry and yet no one seems to, a) be able to name anyone they know who is one and, b) have even the faintest idea of what they do, and I am including in that list several business leaders who employ them.

Alongside this, you have one of my real pet peeves, the job titles that have clearly just been made up, usually by a boss who is trying to be 'cool' but having about as much success as I did when I decided to try hair gel for the first time. A good recent example of this is someone whose CV said that he was 'head of good times' at a tech company. Leaving aside the fact that this sounds like the Facebook status of someone whose entire life peaked in high school, I feel like I have to point out that 'head of bad times' would actually be more impressive. Anyone can run a team when everyone is happy, it is when the chips are down that you want people to step up.

There have been others that have crossed my desk such as 'digital prophet' and 'chief troublemaker' but the one that annoyed me the most was a recent one. It hacked me off so much, that I went back and rewrote this chapter just to include it. It was a job spec that boasted the job title of 'growth ninja'.

This had me gritting my teeth not just because the name is idiotic (though it is), but because ninjas, by definition, are supposed to be stealthy. To put them in charge of growth, which is meant to be one of the louder roles in a business, is just irritating. 'Growth DJ' would genuinely make more sense.

The main danger of ludicrous job titles and incomplete job specs, is people end up doing a role that is a million miles away from what they are supposed to be doing, leading to boredom if it is offering no challenge, and stress and panic if it is too much of a challenge. Plus, more often than not, the increase in stress and panic seems to rarely equate to better salary. This inevitably leads to resignations, increasing the pressure on the team that still remains. It's also ordinarily accompanied by a team member from a certain generation complaining about how Gen Zs just don't know what a hard day's work looks like.

The reality is that job titles and job descriptions are so much more important than the average boss realises. For one thing, they are often the first encounter you might have with a company and, identifying which ones are worth pursuing and which ones should make you run for the hills is one of the best ways to ensure you don't end up having to send me screenshots to read out on social media further down the line.

Job descriptions can typically be broken down into three main sections. The first is the 'About the Company' section which tells you about the broader business you are joining. The second section lists the core requirements of the role, breaking down, in theory, exactly what you will be doing in the job. And finally you have the required skills section – i.e. what you need to have in your back pocket in order to give this role a fair crack.

All of these can cause frustrations by the bucket-load so we will be examining what you should be looking out for that indicates whether the company might be worth joining and which ones have raised the red flag banners and declared war on basic competence.

About the company

How, in all that is holy, do people mess this bit up? All they have to do is provide a little bit of background on the company, what they are trying to do as an organisation over the next few years, and describe the type of people that they are looking to try and recruit. And yet the sheer number of companies and bosses who fall at the very first challenge wouldn't look out of place in an episode of *Squid Game*.

I think the simplicity of that task is part of the issue. It feels like such an easy task that people don't spend that little bit of time actually thinking about it. For one thing, it is nearly always copied and pasted from previous job descriptions with people rarely bothering to read whether it requires updating since the original conception or, even worse, as one company I spoke to the other day confessed to, plainly stolen from a competitor. I know this because they forgot to swap out the competitor's name. This is not the sign of someone who considers this an important part of the recruitment process.

Companies often also fill this section of a job description with phrases that managers think sound great but are ultimately meaningless. 'Solutions provider' or 'thinking outside the box' are particularly popular at the moment but I saw a gardening store talking about requiring someone who can 'handle a high-pressure environment'. With the greatest respect in the world to anyone who works in a gardening store, what is the high-pressure environment you are worried about?

It sounds like I am laying this all on a bit thick and making a bit of a meal of this, but the 'About Us' section is a genuinely good indicator of how seriously a company takes things. If a company doesn't treat it with care, then there will be other areas that are equally half-baked or rushed and an early warning sign that this is not a company you want to commit your working week to.

What you are looking for is a nod to the company's history but with a clear mission. Alongside that, you want a couple of sentences on the type of culture that you will be joining, the type of personalities who do well and the brand values that the company stands by. A good company will be proud of its culture and will want to get that across.

List of duties

TARGETS

If the 'About' section is the appetiser and the 'Required Skills' are the cheese and cigars at the end, then the 'List of Duties' is the meat and two veg. The main course that will define whether you give the meal a positive review or not.

It is also the easiest part of the job spec to interpret and the most accurate when it comes to predicting whether this job or company is the right option for you.

We will get into the specifics of the phrasing of it all shortly, but there are two main parts that you should immediately be on the lookout for. The first is that there needs to be an achievable list of targets and duties. The second is that they need to be trackable, something that you can pick up again in 12 months' time and very easily work out if it has been a successful year or not.

Let's start with the first point. The most obvious reason why this is important is that you need to know what you will be asked to do in order to make the decision as to whether you want to do it in the first place. However, it goes a little deeper than that. A good job spec can be the perfect tool to motivate you for the year. Make it too easy and you run the risk of being bored, too tricky and you will inevitably end up frustrated; what you are looking for is a list of duties which are within your skill set but equally will challenge, but in a way that feels like an exciting stretch, not mission impossible.

You won't be shocked to hear that the latter tends to be more of a problem than the former. Companies frequently take this opportunity to pack this section with duties that are simply not going to happen. And that isn't me being disparaging around the potential efforts you might be willing to put in. I mean, you could put the entire might of the American military behind you and you still would not be able to tick off every duty on some of these job specs. AI in particular has become increasingly bolted on to random job specs as an optimistic punt from companies hoping someone will just miraculously show up and tell them what AI can actually do for them rather than do their own research.

The reason why I am flagging this is that without a clear list of what you need to be achieving, you are doomed to failure before you even start and this will inevitably lead to issues down the road when your boss is marking your homework. It either means a company does not know how much work this role requires, or it doesn't care. Either way, it should be a hard pass for you.

The second part is tracking. One of the worst situations you can find yourself in as an employee, is leaving your end results or targets open to interpretation. While life might be made up of shades of grey, this is an area you damn well want in black and white. Pay rises and performance-related bonuses are almost always tied to meeting targets. Though you'd hope bosses would be reasonable and have your back, the title of this book suggests that this doesn't always happen. You therefore need to make sure that the process to work out whether you've met said targets is crystal clear. Whether or not you have succeeded should be so apparent that not even the world's most gifted legal minds could dispute it.

Phrases to watch out for as a result are things like 'we are looking for someone to significantly increase the revenue of the department'. OK, that sounds great but by how much? What type of revenue? What sort of margin would that require and what resources would I get in order to accomplish this?

The companies that do this best and the ones that get the Ben Askins stamp of approval (don't get excited, that is not as official as it sounds), are those that lay out exactly what they are looking for. 'We are looking for this person to achieve a 25 per cent increase in revenue compared to the last financial year'. 'We want an Account Manager to look after our clients and maintain an 80 per cent retention rate.'

This has the added advantage of also bringing about a legitimate discussion in the interview. Rather than going down the horrendous route of asking inane and pointless 'gotcha' questions, you can then ask around the specifics of the targets and both parties will be able to get a much more accurate feel as to whether this is a relationship that has legs.

The obvious question is what about the roles that aren't directly tied to revenue?

This is where the KPIs (key performance indicators) come

in. Every role will have core duties and you can easily build targets from there. 'This finance role requires accurate and timely forecasting' can easily become 'this finance role requires forecasting that is accurate to within a 3 per cent margin of error and must be completed by the second week of each month'. That is a much more tangible way to approach a role, gives a clear level of expectation and, more importantly, removes any ambiguity as to whether it has been done or not.

The reality is that if a company hasn't thought about any of this then all of the pretty and self-congratulatory sentences they put in the 'About the Company' section starts to feel empty and insincere. It also shows a terrifying lack of understanding of what it takes to make a happy and driven team, because how do you motivate your team if they don't have something to point that motivation at? A job description should be ironclad and, if it isn't, if it feels woolly or thrown together, it is a really good sign that this is not a serious business with whom you want to dedicate the next chunk of your career.

COMPENSATION

There is no bigger red flag to a job spec, boss or company than a salary not being listed within the description. It doesn't matter if it is an exact amount, a range or an upper limit; but there needs to be something.

There are so many reasons why this is an unacceptable thing for a company to do. It is inconsiderate to those applying, frustrating for internal teams, but the reason it gets under my skin like no other is that it is just such a waste of everyone's time.

People know what salary they want, and they are not going to accept taking a job without that information. There might be a few things you can slip past, but what they are going to earn by taking on this job is definitely a number they are going to check. So not being upfront from the beginning is just pointless.

A lot of people will have taken time off work or given up evenings or holidays to interview and when they find out that it was a waste of time and was never going to work due to the pay being below what they are looking for anyway then all it does is lead to anger and frustration. So, what are these companies hoping you might think? That the reason the hiring team hid it shows they really want you? This idea that you can gaslight someone into taking a lower salary is for the birds.

The other idiotic idea is this new trend of companies thinking they can avoid the problem by simply listing the salary as 'competitive'. I can just imagine how pleased the first person who came up with that must have been. It was definitely a marketing agency who started it.

The flaw, in this otherwise genius solution, is obvious. If it is so competitive, then why can't you share proof of it with us? Much like claiming there are benefits to Brexit, you need to at some point cough up proof, otherwise people are just going to stop believing you.

Maybe I am being harsh, maybe the salary they are offering is so 'competitive' that they withhold it so that people who don't work for them don't feel bad about themselves, but it feels unlikely.

The honest truth is the reason why so many companies do this is because they are chancing their arm. Say they have a budget of £45,000 for a role, and someone comes in and says they want

£40,000, companies will happily offer them that amount and consider their work well done for saving £5,000.

The good news is that you don't need to work out if it is incompetence or deviousness that is prompting a company to do this. All you need to know is that if they try this with you then you should be going nowhere near that business.

A range is fine. It is absolutely OK to have a range from say £25,000 – £35,000 as long as the company can be clear about what experience or level of skill is necessary to attain the higher salary.

This leads onto the next stage of this compensation rollercoaster which is how companies list benefits. I don't agree that companies should list all benefits, not least because they can be quite long, however I do think companies should share them as the interview process develops.

What I do object to is bosses doing things like listing holidays under benefits, along with pensions. I appreciate that being pedantic so early in the book is running the risk of you not making it any further but I have to point out that, legally, they have to provide their team with these things, and as soon as something becomes a law you do lose the right to claim credit for following it. If you have a particularly generous scheme then absolutely it is well worth a mention, otherwise you might as well promise that there will be plenty of oxygen in the office with which you can breathe as much as you like.

MANAGEMENT

'You will be reporting to the head of department/ director/ lead team member/ [insert title here]'. That is it. That is all you are looking out for. If a job description has something resembling this then you can consider this section ticked off.

Again, I know that this feels like a frivolous point, but the reason why it is important is that it is part of the wider communication narrative. And if a company hasn't even acknowledged who you might be reporting to, then that just isn't boding well for how they might handle other parts of your interaction with them. I have absolutely zero data to back this up, but I would guess the correlation between companies that forget to have annual reviews and those that don't include this section is depressingly high.

I am also always inherently suspicious about any job spec that says you will report directly to the CEO. Unless you are the CFO or COO, some sort of PA or this is part of an absolutely tiny company, then this just screams of someone who can't let go or delegate. My core belief is that you cannot manage more than five people effectively, and so when random roles are reporting directly to the CEO that just says they haven't gotten their act together structurally, which can only lead to chaos. And speaking as someone who has used the London Underground for over a decade, I consider myself an expert on chaos.

EXCITEMENT

Finally, we have excitement. A job spec shouldn't be just a tedious list of duties that someone has cobbled together frantically after being reminded that they had promised to send it over by the end of the day.

Companies often forget that a job description is the very first piece of correspondence that potential employees will see. At least I hope they forget, because – my word – some of these job descriptions are boring to read. I am not saying they need to be the next Lee Child, but going off some of the more recent efforts I have seen you would get more inspiration reading a set of terms and conditions.

'Passionate', 'thinking outside the box', 'hit the ground running' and all of those other action-packed phrases are the work culture equivalent of populist politicians; they sound great but ultimately lack any sort of substance. 'Thinking outside the box' in particular drives me up the wall. How is that a brag? Why do you have a business where people are spending their days desperately trying to find unusual ways to get anything done? This is not a phrase any competent company or boss should be putting as an essential part of any job. New ideas should always be welcome, but the idea that to get through the day you need to be pulling rabbits out of a hat just to keep things moving sounds terrifying.

The best companies add a little fizz to the proceedings. They talk about areas of the business you will be exposed to, potential new projects you might get a crack at, flag any new skills or training you will personally benefit from. It is OK to get people excited about working for you, and too often this is completely neglected.

Required skills

So we have our list of duties, the core responsibilities that are part of this new challenge, and now we come to the final part of a job description: the required list of skills that the company views as necessary in order to do the job. The implication is that if you do not have these skills, then you need not apply.

But is that true? What are the warning signs that you should be keeping an eye out for?

The first red flag are education requirements. Now before we get into the details of this, I want to make something very clear. I am not undermining education. I am not one of the entrepreneurs who go around saying university is a scam and to avoid it; I think the opposite. There are also lots of impressive people who fully deserve all the plaudits that their hard years of work have delivered as well as a very understandable list of professions that require a significant amount of educational training: doctors, lawyers, accountants, to name but a few.

No, what I am talking about are education requirements that are not relevant or necessary for the job you are applying for.

It is fairly evident why companies do this. Graduate schemes, for example, are frequently overloaded with applications and simply saying 'college degree of x' is an easy way to reduce the amount of CVs you have to review. I personally think you are narrowing your pool of candidates far too early in doing this but that is an argument for another day.

But a lot of companies just seem to wildly inflate the requirements for the job. I was talking to one operations manager who was hiring to fill a role to replace someone who had just left. Despite the seven other people on that team not having a university degree, they listed 'University degree, 2:1 or higher' in the job spec.

They couldn't have more proof that this job could be done

without a degree. In fact, there is an argument that as a degree-wielding candidate is the only data point they didn't have, it was actually the riskier hire. Educational accomplishments can be brilliant indicators that candidates are a great option for a job, but the idea that a lack of them makes a candidate completely unable to do the job has always left a bit of a sour taste in my mouth.

This leads into my least favourite part of an entire job spec. Specifically the 'Nice to haves' section. This, historically, was where you would put a list of skills that aren't absolutely essential but would potentially help you out in either working with the broader organisation or get you up to speed a bit quicker. Experience with specific types of software, for example.

However, this has morphed into a list where managers and companies will stuff every business-sounding word that they can get their hands on that literally no human in the history of mankind would ever be able to tick off. I saw one spec the other day, for an entry level position and, under 'nice to haves', it said 'must feel comfortable in leadership situations'. A very unreasonable expectation of someone in their first ever job I am sure we can all agree. There are six-year-olds in Santa's grotto with less ambitious lists.

Why does this matter? It is just a 'nice to have' anyway, so it won't make a difference. But it does, because this is about patterns, and it is rare that a 'bad boss' or 'bad company' will make just one of these errors and leave it at that. If they are doing this with job descriptions, then they will almost certainly be doing it in other parts of the business, and in creating a list where the majority of requirements are either completely unnecessary or totally impossible, you undermine the legitimate parts of it and either end up attracting the wrong applicants or, even worse, driving away the right ones because they are scared off by a job spec that resembles a drunk groomsman's speech rather than a genuine list of requirements.

The holy grail for this part of job specs, and the sign that a company has a real handle on what they are looking for, is a company that lists a skill level rather than a number of years using that skill. It is way easier to guess 'five years' experience of coding' for example, rather than listing a legitimate level of capabilities.

I am also not enamoured of employers who list 'must have three years' experience in this job role.' What does that even mean? By that logic they could take anyone who has limped over the timeline.

I have always found this laziness (and it really is laziness) frustrating because it is so easy to set your business up as a genuine meritocracy.

A skill level, rather than the number of years required to have used it, is by far the most desirable requirement. If the company does go down the time-based route, it has to, as an absolute minimum, make sense. If the role is an entry level position for example, then they can't start putting 'three years' experience required.'

There was a famous job spec that did the rounds on LinkedIn (where else?) where a guy called Sebastien shared a job spec that was looking for over four years' experience in Fast API. Which all sounded fine until Sebastien pointed out that he had only created FastAPI one and a half years ago. As a general rule, if your manager is ruling out people who actually invented the skills they are looking for because they don't have enough experience, I wouldn't exactly follow them into battle.

Companies that chance their arm by trying to attract a more senior employee than what they actually need are to be avoided for two main reasons. The first is because that level of dishonesty is hardly the bedrock to launch a new professional relationship and secondly, because they are idiots. Even if they do manage to lure a more senior person into the position then they will end up leaving soon after as the role will be too junior for them. Either way, not someone you want to get into business with.

RECRUITMENT & INTERVIEWING

Recruiter: Hi Katherine, just tried to call you. I am sorry to say that you didn't get the job. I just heard from them.

Candidate: Ah that is such a shame, I really thought that it went well. Did they say why?

Recruiter: Yeah, they said they absolutely loved meeting you, but your questions were too financially oriented.

Candidate: What on earth does that mean?

Recruiter: Apparently you asked about money a lot? Is that true?

Candidate: You are joking, is this for real? I asked a couple of questions at the end as I wanted to clarify something around what was included in the benefits package. But for the rest of the interview all of my questions were about the role itself.

Recruiter: Well it seemed to jar. They said they are looking for someone who is more interested in the role rather than all about the money.

When you read exchanges like this, the stat that 58 per cent of people have rejected a job offer due to the poor recruitment experience starts to make a little more sense.

A lot of companies are so bad at interviewing it would be comical if it didn't cause so much anxiety and stress. I had someone message me the other day that she had just gone for a second interview with a company. To be clear, not a second stage interview. It was a fresh first interview, six months after the last one. The manager in question had just forgotten he had interviewed her previously and proceeded to ask her the same questions all over again. The highlight of this story was that apparently, he even made the same joke about her surname. I asked her why she went to the interview for the second time, and she said she was genuinely curious how long it would take for the manager to notice. He never did.

With the bar firmly established, can we please just pause a moment and think about how idiotic the exchange Katherine had was? This company truly seems to be saying that it is not OK to ask about the salary or the benefits of the role that you are directly interviewing for. What is the alternative? You have to go through the entire process and find out at the end? Is it not more helpful for Katherine to make sure that it all works financially for her? To make sure the job ticks the basics sooner rather than later? It will save you getting to the very end of the process where suddenly you realise you are miles apart and all that is left is a waste of everyone's time and an unnecessary lingering resentment.

The question I would love to ask this company is why do you think she was interviewing in the first place? It is, after all, called a job.

The idea that you have to pretend that money isn't a huge driver when you are interviewing for a job is just weird. For some reason, when it comes to interviews, we operate in an alternative reality where we need to pretend that it is the love of the game that is driving you to sign up to the company rather than the basic reality of being a human with bills to pay. Money is of course not the only factor when it comes to a job, but we are kidding ourselves if we think it is not damn well near the top. What is particularly vexing is that there is no commercial benefit to a company being terrible at interviewing. Not only will you miss out on some amazing candidates, but you will also prevent people from applying in the first place. Research shows that 72 per cent of people are likely to share an interview story online if their experience is negative and I know for a fact that that is true because, if it wasn't, my social media channels wouldn't exist and you would not be reading this book today.

The ironic thing is that most companies seem to think they are amazing at recruitment. When asked to back this claim up they conveniently avoid all the usual metrics like retention rate and average length of service and instead pick the more irrelevant KPIs. 'One of our strongest areas is that we are really strict with timings,' one boss told me confidently, 'we never allow an interview to go longer than an hour.' I mean, congratulations? I'd like to find out a little more about what is going on within that very regimented hour before handing out any gold stars.

'We only hire A team players' one boss told me, conveniently neglecting to tell me that his current staff retention rate made my local cricket team's win rate look healthy. Upon closer examination it turned out that his interview approach was to ignore any real job descriptions and to simply 'have a chat' as apparently, he could tell everything simply by 'looking them in the eyes'. Now, while these candidates might have sailed through the 'can hold eye contact' test, it turns out that not discussing what their actual duties are going to be when they get there leaves the door open to miscommunication. A mess from start to finish and one the literal A-Team would have struggled to deliver under. And so that is what this chapter is about. Interviewing. Both why the way we interview is redundant and why companies are so bad at it, and what you can do to make sure you ask the right questions to avoid joining any of these clown shows.

Scan the QR code for an exclusive interview horror story!

The current approach

If you sat down with a blank piece of paper and tried to come up with the most unhelpful formula to hire people, you would land on the modern approach to interviewing. The current average format is a two- or three-stage process. The first stage is the basic qualification. As the recruiter, can you loosely tick off the core list of job requirements? You will not get everything right at this stage, but the idea is that you streamline and find the best few candidates to put through to the next stage. This is often performed by the hiring manager or, in a larger organisation, the HR or recruitment team. The second stage is probably the most important. It is the competency part where, usually the person who will be directly managing the incumbent, asks specific questions to try to really dig into the applicant's experience and skill set. Finally, you explore cultural fit. This is sometimes a conversation with a director in the business, sometimes the CEO or owner. The main purpose of this is just a sanity check to make sure the team up until now have not missed anything completely glaring. It all sounds relatively straightforward when written down like this, yes?

The big problem is that it doesn't mirror any actual job requirements which is always going to impact the accuracy of finding the right person. In every job you will be told what is expected of you, you will get the opportunity to ask any questions or clarifications you need in order to do the job, you will then have a specific deadline and you will then get to deliver the work for that deadline. The modern interview doesn't really touch upon any of that, as far as I can work out; the way most companies approach it, you can discover only two things:

a) Who can carry a conversation
b) Who can think up answers on the fly

To add insult to injury, companies and managers are also deciding that they need to get clever with the questions. They justify it with nonsense lines like 'I want to see how they react under pressure'. In reality, all it does is tell you nothing about the person applying and everything about the person doing the hiring. Please find me a job where a requirement is to try and answer some sort of weird, convoluted riddle. You are hiring a project manager, not looking to take on Gollum in a cave.

One of the strangest examples I have heard about is the interviewer who pulled out a dictionary, opened it at random and pointed at a word and asked the candidate to define it. Now unless you are interviewing for a position on *Countdown*, there is no scenario where that is a useful qualifier. If you are going to do something as pointless as that then at least you could pick a skill that was actually on their CV. That way you might at least discover how honest they are. It really is one of the parts of interviewing that frustrates me the most and, if you think I am overegging this, I have put together a shortlist of the most pointless and ridiculous questions that people have shared to show you exactly what I mean:

1. *If you were a biscuit, what type of biscuit would you be?*

What, in all that is holy, is this question possibly meant to tell you about someone in a job interview? This type of idiocy is particularly common for graduates or junior roles. All those exams, studying, internships, applications and that is the question someone asks you . . .

2. *What is the worst thing that has ever happened to you?*

Yes of course, complete stranger whom I only met five minutes ago and I'm meant to be meeting in some sort of professional setting, let me just walk you through the most traumatic moments of my life.

3. *Have you ever had a physical fight with a co-worker at Thursday night drinks?*

I am sorry, this is too specific a question. This absolutely is something that happened recently, otherwise why name the day?

4. *Do you plan on having kids?*

This would go straight into the same bracket as question 2 under the category 'way too personal'. However, the reason why this gets its own special mention is that this also manages to get the additional tags of 'definitely creepy' and 'also illegal' which is quite an award-winning line-up. You won't be shocked to hear that it was a woman who was on the receiving end of the question.

Finally, just because this topic really does bug me, I have included a clip of me walking you through some of my least favourite questions in even more colourful terms which you can access by scanning the QR code below.

The honest truth is there is no particularly good reason why so many companies and bosses fall down here. One of the big factors is that people aren't really taught why they should be asking certain questions and also why they aren't allowed to ask others. The lack of training in regards to how to conduct an interview not only causes issues with people making basic hiring mistakes but it leads to additional problems where people start developing their own style, resulting in a lack of consistency across the whole business.

Alongside this, problems arise when hiring managers try to educate themselves. There isn't much in the way of formal qualifications or accreditations when it comes to interviewing and recruitment and, without that as at least a starting point, people will frequently turn to the internet for help which, depending where you end up, can lead to further problems. I remember one hiring manager, who, with the best intentions in the world, copied an interviewing strategy without realising it had come from a Crypto bro who had never hired anyone in his life.

The final part of this is companies not preparing for the interview. This is a trend that steadily worsens as you go up the seniority ladder. I am sure I'm not the only one to have witnessed a founder or CEO join an interview without even knowing the name of the person they are meeting, let alone looking at their profile to work out which areas of the business they are meant to join.

The solutions

So, as a candidate, what can you do when you are being interviewed? The good news is that you have a lot more power than you think, especially when it comes to weeding out the incompetent companies and making sure you pick the right company for you. If you are only going to take one piece of advice from this whole chapter it is this: an interview is about the company selling to you as much as you need to sell yourself to them. Use that time to ask the questions and gather the answers that you need to work out if it is the right place for you.

A company that feels like they are investing in a sensible process is likely going to invest in you. It is really important to think about what you can do to make sure you don't end up like Katherine or any other of the examples I have listed. Before you agree to the interview, do your research. Reddit, Twitter/X, Glassdoor, LinkedIn: these are all great places to start. Don't be afraid to reach out to people who have recently left the company to ask what it was like. Have a look on LinkedIn at the current employees and see if you have any connections in common. I truly believe that there is the right company out there for everyone, but it is unlikely to just fall into your lap, and so it is important you take the time to look around. Funny interview stories are great for dinner parties further down the line, but when you are in the midst of one, and you are worried about your next job or the next stage in your career, it can be an awful place to be.

The final thing I would say is if you are in the middle of a shocking interview, you do not have to stay for the whole thing. You really don't. It is an interview not a police interrogation and, as such, you are completely within your rights to simply stop the interview and call it there.

'I am so sorry, but the last thing I want is to waste your time and I don't think that this is the right fit for me and so I don't think it is worth continuing with the interview' is all you need to say. You should never feel like you have to sit there and suffer.

But when the interview is going well and you want to make sure you take advantage of this opportunity to find out about them and whether they're right for you, here are some of the best questions that you can ask:

1. *Is there anything that might happen in the next six–twelve months which might impact my role?*

When it comes to job security, you are at your most vulnerable in the first few months of your new role. Not only because you are still likely to be in your probation period but also because 'last in, first out' is a very real principle in many businesses. Even if you are phenomenal at the role, if external factors impact the business in some way and they are forced to make cuts, you will very likely be on the shortlist. Alongside this, there may be internal plans in the works such as merging teams together, reorganising duties or plans to deprioritise services or products that might be key to your role. This question reduces the risk of being completely blindsided. That is not to say companies are always entirely honest, but they may give a clue as to what the potential plans are for the coming months and how that might impact you.

2. *Is the company currently profitable? If so, what is the current profit per cent?(If the answer is no, then make sure you ask what the current burn rate – the rate at which a company is spending its cash reserves – is.)*

This is a great question for two main reasons. The first is obvious. How secure is the company and, by default, your role in said company? There is no point quitting your job only to join a business that is all set to fail within the next few months. The reason why you want to ask this as a per cent rather than an amount is because a per cent margin is a much better indicator. £1 million profit sounds amazing, but if the business is doing £100 million in revenue then that is only a 1 per cent profit margin making the business incredibly precarious and hinting that they're potentially considering reducing costs. Anything in the 20 per cent plus bracket can make you feel reasonably secure. Equally, from a burn rate perspective, it can take a while for a company to become profitable, especially if their model is around growth. However, if they have less than 12 months' worth of outgoings in the bank I would really weigh up the pros and cons of joining.

The second reason why this is a good question is because if they do not know these numbers or are unwilling to share, then this is an enormous red flag. There is no reason not to share these types of numbers in a business unless they have a culture of secrecy and mistrust. If they do not know, then that is almost worse. It is damn well their job to know. If they can't answer basic figures like this then where else are they dropping the ball?

3. What is the company's vision for the next five years?

What are we all going to be trying to achieve? Revenue and money are all well and good and will always be part of the mission, but a business is unlikely to grow on that and that alone. The successful businesses, and the ones that can really supercharge your career, always have something else. It could be something specific like Amazon who want 'to be Earth's most customer-centric company; to build a place where people can come to find and discover anything they might want to buy online' or it can be broader like Apple's 'to make the best products on Earth, and to leave the world better than we found it'. But every good business will have one and will be able to summarise it succinctly. If you ask this question and they are still rambling five minutes later then that doesn't count.

4. If I was successful in this role, what would progression potentially look like?

Is there a future for you in the long term? And, more importantly, is this role going to give you the next step in your career? It is OK to be a little bit selfish and ask questions like this. The interview is for you as much as it is for the company and making sure it ticks the boxes for what you are looking for is important.

One of the best signs is to be told about the person who had your job before. If they have gone on to bigger and better things, then you can view that as very encouraging as to whether it will benefit you as well.

5. How would you describe the culture of the business?

There are a lot of ways that this can be answered in a positive way. The trick is to listen out for all those phrases that companies think are positives but are in fact significant red flags. If you are in an interview and someone uses the phrase 'we work hard, play hard' then run for the hills. You can almost guarantee that this business overworks everyone and then tries to hide that fact by serving ridiculous amounts of alcohol every Thursday and Friday. Similar to anyone saying 'We are like a family here'. It basically means that they will happily wield guilt and manipulation to get you to go above and beyond your employment contract with zero additional pay. The other phrases that I would keep a careful ear out for are anything along the lines of 'we have a very flat structure' or 'we like to think outside the box'. With the former, you can be confident that you are dealing with a very toxic blame culture and the latter is code for making the business up on the fly as you go along. I am all for the odd moment of inspiration, but the core of a business should be very much in control and inside the box.

6. *What is the biggest challenge facing the team I am joining?*

You might think that the ideal answer to this question would be 'absolutely nothing, it is an incredible team to be joining'. However, trust me when I tell you that this is an enormous red flag for the simple reason there is no such thing as a perfect team. It has never existed and never will. Even the Avengers had their flaws. Any company that responds to this question by saying 'there are none' is either lying to you or completely deluded. Neither scenario bodes well for your next career move. What you are looking for here is an honest assessment of the challenges, along with a plan of action on how to fix them. 'The team are great, but they definitely have too much on at the moment and so we are starting to see an impact in the quality of the work which is why we are hiring for this role.'

Or 'We've had a couple of competitors take some of the market share for this particular department, however we have revamped the marketing budget and are looking to roll out a big push over the next six months to get back on track'. Simple acknowledgement of the challenge with a plan of action, that is the sweet spot for something like this. I feel also obliged to point out that, if the challenges are completely horrific then that doesn't outweigh any honesty points. You would think I didn't have to say this, but I received a story recently where the interviewer openly admitted that they had so many open roles because of how many people had been let go or quit due to systemic sexual harassment from some senior figures in the business.

All of these questions are ones that a good company should be able to answer easily. Any sort of floundering is a red flag. It is so important to use the time that you have to ask the questions that you need the answers to. Ignore all the misguided advice on 'not asking about money'. This is your time to really dig down, and it's important you take advantage of it.

The big issue you have with companies who deploy some of these more toxic or silly approaches to interviewing and recruitment, is that these are very unlikely to be the only silly or toxic thing that they do. Pay attention during the recruitment stage of joining a company. It is not a perfect science, but they can genuinely give you some really accurate signals as to whether you are joining a professional and engaged business or a complete farce cobbled together by hot air and bullshit.

The truth of the matter is that interviewing should not be causing the number of problems between employees and bosses that it seems to be doing. The slightest investment in training, or making sure hiring managers have enough time to properly prep for each interview would make such a difference to how so many companies approach this side of things. But there are plenty of companies and bosses who do interviews extremely well. And if you ever become a hiring manager or hope to one day be recruiting for a role, here are the two main strategies that, from my side, have always worked best:

1. **Sharing the types of questions that you are going to ask ahead of time.**

I know this seems counterproductive, but I think this is a far better way to find out who will be the best fit for the role. Think about what it is you are looking for. You want someone who will take the request seriously, will do their preparation, will present the answers you asked them to look into, and then answer any questions that you might have. I challenge anyone to look me in the eye and tell me that that is not a more valid method to identify who might be a better fit for your company, rather than watching someone flounder trying to work out if they should say their favourite biscuit is a Hobnob or a Digestive.

2. **Introducing a task element into the process.**

This second part is used a little more often, and is a great way to really dig into someone's competencies and gives you a chance to ask relevant questions about why they did something a certain way etc. The only thing I would add to this is that sometimes companies take it too far and set a ludicrous amount of work for these tasks. If they are going to take more than an hour and a half the only fair thing to do would be to pay for the time. That way you are being fairly compensated as the interviewee and, from a business perspective, you can ensure that the candidate takes the job seriously. I was sent one horror story where someone planned out an entire campaign and the company simply took the work, rejected the candidate and implemented the campaign in full without paying them anything.

COMPANY CULTURE

Boss: Hi all,

Hope everyone had a great time last night. I don't know about you all but my head is feeling awful :(

The total bill in the end came to just over $1,100 which means that you each owe me about $110. Can you all please send me your share before the end of the day?

Thanks,
Chris

Employee: Hey Chris,

Sorry I am a bit confused here, I thought you said the company was covering the bill. Why are we now being asked to pay?

Thanks,
Chloe

Boss: Hi Chloe,

So sadly we went over the budget and we have to cover the difference. The price of a good time I guess lol!

Employee: Hi Chris,

But I didn't really drink anything? I only had one or two and so I don't understand why I have to pay so much?

Boss: Hey Chloe,

This isn't about 'who drank what', this is about us being a team. If you don't pay I am going to have to simply take it off your wages on next pay day.

Employee: Hi Chris,

You are not allowed to do that. And if you try to do that I will go straight to HR. You and Michael were the two who abused the bar bill and, while I am happy to pay my share, I am not paying for all of your drinks. I have spoken to the rest of the team and they are in complete agreement.

No one thinks having a good culture is a bad thing. Of course they don't. It is one of the few things that everyone is in total agreement on, from the most successful and powerful of CEOs to unpaid interns. And I am not being hyperbolic when I say *total* agreement. According to research done by Deloitte, 94 per cent of entrepreneurs and business leaders say that a good culture is critical to success. That's a whopping 94 per cent! In a Twitter/X-fuelled world of misinformation, you don't even get that many people agreeing that the world is round.

It goes even further. TeamStage, the people behind a cloud-based management software, did some analysis that said that having a highly engaged team can lead to a 202 per cent increase in production and having a culture that attracts high performing candidates can lead to a 33 per cent increase in revenue. Do you know how much companies spend on sales, marketing, RnD and everything in between to just get a fraction of that sort of increase?

And yet this is where we get to the disconnect. Just because you have a bad manager, doesn't mean that you necessarily have a manager promoting a toxic culture. There are plenty of examples where you can point at a situation where a manager was poor without saying they have created a toxic workplace. But if these numbers are even remotely true, how has culture managed to get a chapter in this book? Why do 75 per cent of all employees say they have experienced a toxic work culture? And why is my inbox groaning with stories from people complaining about how awful their boss is and how terrible the working environment they have created is?

I know the easy answer is to say that this is just classic business, they don't care about you and the boot of capitalism will slowly grind you down until there is nothing left but dust. (Before anyone thinks that I am getting particularly poetic, I have borrowed this line directly from a comment on one of my recent videos.) And of course, you can find examples of this, but when companies do step over the line it is because there is also a financial reason behind doing so. Companies are very consistent. For example, easyJet claiming that the reason they charge for extra luggage is 'for safety reasons', is objectively nonsense, but you can at least see the very poorly hidden financial incentive to come up with said nonsense.

But when it comes to culture that is not the case. If the numbers above are correct, then having a good culture is one of the easiest and quickest ways to achieve financial success. Even the most narcissistic of bosses recognises this and should be motivated to at least have a go at creating one. And yet we live and work in a world where, on the surface at least, companies are doing everything they can to not participate in building healthy company cultures.

There are two main reasons for this. The first is that there is a genuine misunderstanding of what a good culture is. The second is that, even when a company does understand what a good culture is, they demonstrate spectacularly poor efforts when it comes to implementing it. This chapter will look at exactly where bosses and companies are going wrong and also, how you, as an employee, can help identify exactly what a good company culture looks like and what the warning signs are to help you avoid the absolute shockers.

Disconnect

Let's start with problem one: when people don't understand what culture is. 'I don't have time for all of that, and neither does my team', one boss declared to me, 'long hours and elbow grease is how we got where we are, and it is how we will keep growing.'

It was very apparent that he didn't have the first idea as to whether his team did in fact have time for it, as he very clearly had not asked them. The irony of his own statement also made a slight whistling noise as it soared over his head, because in describing a business that had an extremely hard-working approach, he was describing, yep you guessed it, a culture.

At a basic level, there are two main parts to a company culture. There is the mission of the company, which is what you are all trying to do. And then you have the written and unwritten rules of how everyone goes about achieving said mission.

The best missions are those that are incredibly simple and can be defined in just one sentence. 'To organise the world's information and make it universally accessible and useful' is a great example from Google. Nike has 'to bring inspiration and innovation to every athlete in the world.' A very clear statement that gives everyone an innate understanding of what the purpose of the business is.

But brands with clear statements are the exceptions. I was once shown a company mission that was two and a half pages long and the wording was so complicated it looked like the boss in question was going for a Scrabble record rather than trying to summarise his company's goal.

You will notice that the best companies do not go near the topic of money when it comes to company missions. Of course, profit and revenue are going to be the key cornerstone of everything a company does. But when it comes to culture, it is all about getting people to buy into the mission and they need more purpose than simply adding value to share prices and driving up profit margins. Not least because employees rarely benefit in any meaningful way from this.

I had one CEO who told me the company mission was to achieve a seven-figure profit before he turned 40. Not his own personal mission, his actual company mission. And he was wondering why people weren't buying into it. He might as well have changed the statement to 'aiming to purchase the boss a villa in Tuscany by 2027.'

And nothing shows more company cultural ignorance than the way a company utilises and brags about their benefits and perks. 'We have a fantastic company because we pay for massive bar bills every Thursday' just doesn't do what so many people seem to think it does.

Now don't get me wrong, team socials where everyone goes out and has a good time is absolutely a great thing to do. However, you need to recognise that perks and benefits should be used to enhance the existing company culture, not simply used as a culture in its own right. Doing random gestures of inconsistent generosity is not going to build the high-performance company everyone always says that they want.

In fact, some perks have the opposite effect and can damage your culture, even though technically you are doing something nice. Sephora, the beauty retail giant, set an early bar when, upon achieving $10 billion in revenue they bought everyone cookies with the words '$10 billion' on, which led to a very predictable backlash.

Another memorable example, this time from one of my followers, was the person who told me that, as a thank you for working so hard during the Covid crisis, the company bought their team a box of six Capri-Sun to share. The worst part about it? There were eight of them. Asking a toddler to share a juice box will go down badly, asking a grown adult is just a metaphorical slap in the face. That is the inherent problem with not having any real plan and instead relying on random perks. Some of them will land, and some of them will not.

Another big reason employees can get hacked off with their bosses and companies is the disconnect between external communications of said company culture to the world and what happens in reality. One story shared with me included the boss frequently publishing posts on LinkedIn talking about the importance of making mistakes and treating them as an opportunity for growth, while it was widely known internally at his company that the second anything went wrong he would name and shame the 'culprit' in front of everyone.

This isn't unusual, for the very simple reason that words are cheap when it comes to building a culture, and everyone is fully aware of this. The big question comes as to whether your boss actually backs up what they tell everyone when it really matters. That is what a good culture entails, otherwise bosses find themselves with the word 'hypocrite' settled in between a couple of juicier adjectives that I don't think my agent is going to let me print in this book. The simple fact of the matter is if a company is saying things on their social channels, or website or any other marketing collateral that completely jar with reality, then you are going to create a feeling of mistrust. To be clear, I am not talking about exaggeration or spin, I am talking about the direct contradictions.

Finally, there's the top-down issues. Specifically, company leaders and those who are the most senior thinking they can get away with not doing the things that juniors are expected to do. Now, no one is going to pretend that being at the top or near the top of the food chain doesn't come with some benefits but when it comes to establishing a culture, either everyone needs to commit or no one does. This is the one and only time in my life where I will compare myself to the US Marines: 'no person left behind' is the motto of culture.

'All of our time is to be respected', says the CEO who is 15 minutes late to every single meeting he ever attends. 'We make sure that team members don't message each other on annual leave', says the boss who just fired off a WhatsApp asking 'just a quick question' to their employee who is currently travelling to Spain. Both saying all the right things, both completely missing the point.

Green flags and warning signs

With that in mind, let's explore the nine main elements that make up company culture and look at the green and red flags for each one so that you can understand whether the place you currently work deserves you and whether the company you are applying for is the right fit.

COMMUNICATION

If I was asked what the most important part of establishing a high-performance culture in a business was, communication would be at the very top of the list.

The single biggest sign that a company takes this seriously and is doing it well is when the communication happens both ways. One boss that I knew spent a huge amount of time telling everyone how important feedback was and then promptly banned exit interviews because he didn't like what someone had said about the company. Alongside this quite impressive level of small mindedness, he also had a big poster put up 'When I say jump, you say "how high".' This might not feel like the most relevant detail but he had the absolute audacity to call this a motivational poster and so I felt it had to get a small mention to really round out the corners of this particular boss's personality for you.

Now this approach to communication would be somewhat effective if humans were perfect and no mistakes were ever made. But sadly, we haven't quite mastered that yet as a species and this idea that a manager or a boss can have an effective culture without ever getting feedback from people more junior than them is just deluded.

The best companies have regimented communication structures where people get an opportunity to directly ask questions as well as voice any concerns or worries. Good examples of this are having a one-to-one meeting with your manager once a fortnight, having monthly team meetings to go through areas in more detail and, if you are part of a much bigger organisation, a quarterly presentation by the senior team talking about where the opportunities are and what the challenges are.

The latter is particularly important, because the biggest red flag to watch out for are those bosses and companies that keep their teams completely in the dark as to what is going on. I am of course not saying junior employees need to be told everything as soon as anything of note happens, but keeping people abreast of what is going well and where the business is struggling is essential. As a manager, this will help you in the long run because if you have explained that the company is struggling and walked through the plan to get back on track, people will be a lot more understanding if you have to make tough decisions over things like bonuses and pay rises.

EMPLOYEE RECOGNITION AND APPRECIATION

If the company you work at wins, do you win? That is the only question to ask when it comes to employee recognition and appreciation. The best companies recognise that the only honest way to show their appreciation is that, when the company does well financially, they put their hands in their pocket.

There are a variety of ways to do this. It can be in the form of a bonus, or it can be done through profit share schemes.

If companies do not offer this, then they do not get to claim they show their employees any sort of appreciation. It really is as simple as that. Everything else is just noise. I have seen companies bend over backwards doing absolutely everything they could to walk the line where they get to claim they appreciate their team but not actually incentivise them – and it just doesn't work. Sharing the good times allows you to build up the credit to get through the bad.

When it comes to recognition, financial rewards are always going to be the most appreciated. I am also a big believer in public praise, and any company that celebrates its employees publicly is one that gets a green flag next to its name. One of the biggest tests though is how middle management deals with recognition. One of the worst things you can have in a culture is managers stealing or hogging the limelight for themselves. As a manager, if your team does well you get the credit anyway, so all you are doing in stealing credit from those below you is hacking them off, leading to them being less productive and ending up with less credit to steal in the first place.

The best companies genuinely celebrate other people's wins, and they have mechanisms and processes in place where people who do good work are recognised for it.

WORK–LIFE BALANCE

People always assume I hate businesses that have bosses who pride themselves on their lack of work–life balance. They think that I have a dart board with the face of every boss who dares to say 'we often have to work weekends or work evenings, that is just how we do it', but I really don't.

As long as you are honest with the people you hire and your existing team, I don't care if you try to make them fully available 24 hours a day and expect them to work a double shift on Christmas Day.

I don't agree with that approach. I have always felt having that balance is key. However, if a boss wants to set his business up like that, is upfront about the demands and the team doesn't get any nasty surprises, then I am all for it. The people who interview for that business can tell them to 'do one' if that approach to work is not for them.

The bosses you have to watch out for, and the biggest red flags, are the ones that pretend they have a phenomenal respect for work–life balance in the interview and then do everything in their power to show you just what a sucker you were for believing them.

Honesty is the only benchmark of note here. The best companies provide an honest account of their expectations and give you all of the facts to make your decision.

PROFESSIONAL DEVELOPMENT

Feeling like you are doing the same thing over and over is one of the most dispiriting feelings in the workplace. One of the quicker ways to damage company culture is to leave staff feeling that they are treading water with very little opportunity to try something new or develop their existing skill sets.

It is a delicate balance that you are looking for. If everything is new and challenging and there doesn't feel like there is much support then you can quickly feel overwhelmed, but if everything is completely easy and you haven't been pushed at all, work can feel tedious and demotivating.

The sweet spot is somewhere in the middle. The ratio I like to use is 80/20; you should feel confident in doing 80 per cent of your job, with 20 per cent feeling new or challenging. You should always feel your job is pushing you but in a 'you can do it' kind of way, rather than simply pushing you off a cliff and being told to flap your arms.

One of the easiest ways to work out if your boss takes this seriously or not is to ask what the training budget is. Every company should have one, whether that is for external activities like conferences or internally focused workshops and courses. If a company doesn't have one, that is a pretty good indicator as to how important they consider this part of a working culture.

Another good question is to ask how many people each manager is in charge of. This is the most important indicator as to how your development journey will be in your job, because if this person is managing 20 different people, you can be very confident that you simply will not get anywhere near the required TLC to achieve what you are looking for. I have a hard rule to make sure that no one is managing more than five people directly. Any more, and they simply can't give the required time to develop and train you.

The final indicator that I look out for is whether people have a list of development areas they need to focus on. 'They never learn' one boss moaned at me once, who, upon being asked if his employees knew what they were meant to be learning, crumpled like wet tissue paper. The whole point of development areas and training is that you don't know what you don't know, and it is firmly on your manager, supported by the business, to provide that training. Too often I see companies treat 'time for managers to train their team' with the same level of respect that they would for their employees' side hustle.

INCLUSION AND DIVERSITY

Now I am fully aware that if you rolled Brexit, Net Zero and Critical Race Theory into one culture-war blob you still wouldn't come close to the amount of complaints I see about inclusion and diversity.

This section is not about quotas, or how qualified people supposedly miss out on jobs so that unqualified people from certain backgrounds can be employed instead. That is simply not what that means. I am talking about whether the culture of a business means that everyone in the company feels comfortable talking. Junior or senior, introvert or extrovert, male or female, the best businesses encourage everyone to speak up, whether it is coming up with a new idea, or raising potential issues, or providing solutions to challenges.

The fact that diversity and inclusivity has been bastardised to fuel the ever-hungry culture wars is increasingly frustrating because people now believe it to be something that it just simply isn't.

You see, the value of diversity and inclusion makes sense when you think about it. If you have ten people in a room, but only two of them feel comfortable raising problems, ideas or anything in between, then you are only utilising 20 per cent of your team's potential. It is probably also more like 15 per cent due to the fact that, inevitably, the loudest voice very rarely has the most useful contribution.

A great question to ask at interviews is how people collaborate in the business. Is it once a month in an intimidating boardroom with a slightly impatient director who isn't across his brief or is the company more aware that some people require additional support in order to coax the best out of them? One-to-one meetings, workshops off site, rules around team meetings where everyone has to come up with one idea that is monitored by someone senior. All of these are great options to help get the best out of your team.

Finally, it is useful to have people from a range of different backgrounds and skill sets, for the obvious reason that the more diverse a group of people in the room, the bigger the range of ideas and solutions you might be able to come up with. I had one complete berk of a boss who shared with me on social media that he refused to hire someone unless they had a six pack.

Moving past the obvious point that a six pack is hardly indicative as to whether you can work in an office, he genuinely didn't seem to realise how obviously he was favouring men of a relatively young age and if your entire team is made up of the exact same demographic, those 'out of the box' solutions you all bang on about are not going to be as accessible as you might think.

TEAM COLLABORATION AND SUPPORT

The most interesting thing about this part of a company culture is that every business in the world claims they are good at this bit with no real evidence to support said claim. This is much like the truly amazing stat that 46 per cent of men in the world think that, if it came down to it, they could land an aeroplane in distress.

When it comes to collaboration and support, words are completely meaningless. It is all about what your boss actually does that reveals all.

One of the best ways to gauge how worthy they are of the 'good culture' title is their approach to new starters. Do they look after them and give them a chance to get their feet on the ground or do they just toss them a few angry clients and expect them to figure it all out? Things like assigning new starters a buddy when they join the business so that they have a friendly face to ask questions of. Providing a lunch mate for the first week. These are basic things that can make a huge difference.

I was given a painful reminder of this by a story shared with me where the boss had genuinely forgotten that a new starter had joined. I am not saying that the first day had slipped his mind, I mean he had actually forgotten them. Forgotten he had hired them, forgotten that they even existed. And so, when they showed up for the first day there was no structure in place, no plans and this poor individual was left twiddling their thumbs as this 'exciting new opportunity for their career' which was a direct quote when they were offered the role, didn't exactly get off to a flying start.

I don't care how much free beer you offer, you do not get to claim you support your team if you have forgotten they exist. Another great way to gauge whether your company is truly supportive is how they approach recruitment in general. One of the most common complaints I get is people reporting that their boss either doesn't believe them or just brushes off concerns that they need additional hires and support to either replace people who have left or to handle an increased workload due to new clients or projects.

I cannot overemphasise how much of a red flag this is, especially when your boss is ignoring direct evidence of the requirement such as time sheets and volume of work. They also get a bonus if they try and justify their refusal through meaningless motivational slogans such as 'we all just need to dig deep' and, 'I know that you can handle this.' It shows such a fundamental lack of respect. One of the best pieces of advice I can give to avoid this exact type of boss is by ducking any job advert you see with the phrase 'we need this candidate to hit the ground running'. You do not need Einstein to break that particular code which is 'we should have hired a couple of months earlier and now we are in a bind.'

Another red flag to watch out for that hints a company isn't as supportive of their staff as they would like you to think, is how they handle unexpected absences or personal issues. The boss who just assumes you are lying when you say you are sick, especially when it is something that has never happened before, is never a good thing. The same applies for when personal tragedy impacts your life and your boss treats it as nothing more than an inconvenience for them. I had one memorable call on my YouTube show where, while a family member was dying, a follower had to deal with his boss calling him seven times asking when he thought he would be back into work.

I do have some good news: the best bosses and managers are easy to spot, because they practise what they preach. Providing clear support channels for when you are struggling, and actually listening to the feedback. Having proper onboarding plans for new starters. Showing basic empathy for when things happen in your life and being proactive about helping, such as taking on some of your workload or providing additional flexibility to help get you through it. Actions really do speak louder than words.

POSITIVE WORK ENVIRONMENT

'I like my job' is the biggest green flag you can ever ask for, which is a bit sad when you think about it. Enjoying your job feels like it should be a bit of a baseline. The bare minimum with which we should then be building on. In fact, only about 49 per cent of people enjoy their job. Now, I feel like I need to determine what I mean by that. There is no job that exists where you spend the day floating around on cloud nine. Every job has its tough moments. But if you take a six-month snapshot, you should estimate that you were happy with your job about 75 per cent of the time.

Listening to your gut is the best barometer you have when it comes to working out if the company you are in is the right place for you. Because there is something awful about being miserable at work. And I am not talking about 'I have a tough deadline' or 'that customer is just being such a pain'. I am talking about that pit of the stomach feeling that just makes even getting out of bed tough and fills you with absolute dread on Sunday evening.

One of the quickest ways to trash a company culture is to allow bullies and people who genuinely make other people's lives miserable to remain in their place. This is amplified a thousand-fold when the person in question is responsible for managing other people. One of the best signs to look out for is whether the team you are joining or part of has seen a huge turnover recently. The Frontline Leader Project points out that 57 per cent of people who quit their job do so because of their boss, and if several people leave one team in quick succession, you can bet a huge amount of money that someone in a position of seniority is to blame.

One of the most positive signs that a company takes working culture seriously is how HR responds to complaints about people in a position of seniority. Do they take complaints seriously and investigate? Do people who are found to have behaved terribly get formally reprimanded?

If it is an open secret that a particular figure who is senior behaves terribly, and no one does anything about it, run for the hills.

Toxic people, much like in life, can ruin even the best job or workplace and, if your company shows that it won't take the necessary action to rectify it then the only thing you can do is leave.

TRANSPARENCY AND ACCOUNTABILITY

Leadership at work has always interested me. And the reason being is that, as a talent, it has always appeared to somehow be both overrated and underrated all at the same time.

When times are good, anyone can be in charge. You could simply leave an empty chair in the CEO's office and the ship will more or less drive itself. In fact, going off some of the stories so far, I might be doing the empty chair a disservice.

And the reason I say that is if everyone is happy, enjoying their role, projects are running smoothly, clients are all raving about your company's work, then often the worst thing you can do as a leader is dip your oar in for the sake of scratching the 'I am important and should be involved' itch. The best leaders know that, sometimes, you just need to clear the way in front, and let the people who know what they are doing take charge.

It is also completely underrated because 'leader' becomes the single most important role in the office when things are tough. How a boss handles bad news or mistakes in the office is the best indicator of whether they are worthy of the phrase 'good boss'.

One of the more surprising good signs of a great boss is one that is willing to make the tough call and fire people, especially those at a more senior level. The worst-case scenario is a business where toxic people are allowed to linger like a tuna salad in the fridge that 'you will definitely eat tomorrow'. A boss who can and will remove them, putting the culture of the business first, is one you will, more often than not, be very willing to work for.

PURPOSE-DRIVEN WORK

Everyone knows the main reason you go to work is for the salary. However, the best bosses recognise that there needs to be something more than that, a common purpose which brings the team together. It can be the quality of the work, a social purpose, or it can be based around innovation. Whatever it might be, it needs to provide something more.

It isn't like every company needs to be saving the world, but feeling proud of your work is such a powerful addition to a business culture. A company that can easily and eloquently describe what their purpose is, is a massive green flag in my book.

ANNUAL LEAVE

Boss: *Hey, where are you? I just need to run through something with you.*

Employee: *I am on annual leave today, literally on the plane as I text you!*

Boss: *Are you actually??? Did I know about this? What about the call this afternoon with Stephen?*

Employee: *I honestly have no idea what you are talking about.*

Boss: *I sent you an email this morning about Stephen wanting to chat about the campaign.*

Employee: *I haven't checked email, did you not get my OOO?*

Boss: *I didn't clock that. I know this is a big ask, but can you jump on the call? It is in a few minutes.*

Employee: *No. I am literally on the plane about to take off!*

Boss: *You are really leaving me in the lurch here.*

People absent from work, on days they are expected to be working, is a tale so old you can trace it back to the building of the pyramids. That is not me employing artistic licence. There is literally a stone tablet found in Egypt dating back to 1,250 BC that details a list of complaints about people missing work because of things going on in their personal life. My personal favourite on the list? Someone couldn't make it in because they had 'been drinking with Khonsu'. Whether Khonsu was such a big name that this was a legitimate excuse, or the employee in question was simply banking on the truth being the best way forward, is a question that will sadly remain unanswered.

The other one that caught my eye was that 'scorpion sting' was listed over 100 times. Was this as big a threat as the tablet suggested? Or was this just the ancient Egyptian equivalent of 'food poisoning', the go-to excuse for when you woke up feeling rough having had a big evening with Khonsu and the boys? 'Sorry boss, that damn scorpion got me again, should hopefully have shaken it off by tomorrow but will keep you posted.'

If the concept of not working on days we are supposed to is ancient, the reverse phenomenon of being made to work on days we are *not* meant to is a more modern occurrence.

Annual leave is one of the most frequent causes of friction between employees and bosses. It is the 'new money' of workplace problems, and it is seriously starting to flash the cash in a way that would make the most Crypto bro of bros blush.

The core problem behind why it is such a combustible issue, and why my inbox is filled with so many stories, comes down to employees (quite rightly) viewing annual leave as a right, whereas a lot of leaders or managers (quite wrongly) seem to view it as some sort of privilege. One that they believe they should have a right to mess with if it starts to become an inconvenience for them. When you are starting from such different positions, you are always going to get into trouble.

But that is not why it has become such a supercharged problem over the last few years. In the UK, annual leave has been compulsory and a right for employees since 1938 and it never had the teeth that it does today. If you don't believe just how recent and sharply this problem has exploded, then I refer you to a YouGov poll in 2015 that showed that a quarter of workers were contacted by their boss on annual leave. By 2021 that number had increased to 75 per cent. That is a meteoric rise. Which begs the question, what has changed for it to become such a problem?

The more observant of you will already be pointing out that technology is the obvious culprit. You could also make the point that me going back to the building of the pyramids was unnecessary to arrive at that conclusion but then you wouldn't have got to hear about Khonsu's drinking exploits and I think you can agree your world would be a lesser place because of it. But what has technology done that has caused such a plethora of issues with how bosses and managers are interacting with their employees? For all the stories and examples that I have been sent, it all boils down to the combination of two things: bosses thinking they have the right to hit up their employees no matter where they are in the world, and technology making it depressingly easy for them to do so.

Technology has been the petrol on this particular workplace fire. There has been a gradual increase over the last few decades as technology has advanced. Everyone starting to have their own mobile phones was an obvious turning point; the arrival of the BlackBerry and having access to your emails via your phone for the first time was another, but we have reached full 24/7 contact mania.

And there is no scenario where improved technology is not to blame for this, both in how we use it while we are at work and the ease with which you can get hold of people when they are not there. It's not that employees didn't have bosses who were just as bad in previous decades, of course they did. But they just had an easier time of achieving plausible deniability around why their boss hadn't been able to get hold of them.

Plausible deniability is the key to this whole chapter and why annual leave has become such an issue. The most common comment I get on social media when I share stories about this topic is 'why don't you just ignore them'. In an ideal world that would be the solution. But it isn't that easy for two main reasons. The first is that any boss who is going to such lengths to get hold of you during annual leave is almost guaranteed to be in the 'arsehole' category and so the potential repercussions of what might happen when you come back to work if you ignore them really do loom large. They can truly make your life miserable and so while you might get a couple of days' breather by simply ignoring them, you know that you could be facing a truly miserable time when you get back. An American lawyer came forward to share a story with me via my YouTube channel show. Even though she worked every day on her holiday, apart from one when she was on a hike with her family and so had limited signal, she still got screamed at because she had, and I quote, 'let the side down'.

The second reason it's not easy to ignore them is the stress. Even if you are not responding, if your phone is pinging off every other minute it just keeps you constantly on edge and thinking about work. Which, the more astute of you will recognise, is not really what a holiday is meant to be doing. You end up in this weird scenario where it would have been easier and more restful to just not be on holiday in the first place, which even the most hard-core believer in work ethic must acknowledge doesn't feel like the healthiest attitude.

And this wasn't as much of an issue in the past. Early iterations of mobiles lost signal the second a cloud appeared and most upper management viewed emails on phones as some sort of witchcraft. This allowed you to be able to pretend that you weren't aware they were trying to get hold of you, even if they tried and, because a lot of bosses of that era required three juniors just to turn their computer on, they often just didn't bother in the first place.

By contrast, it is borderline alarming how easy it is to get hold of people now. Here are the different routes of attack that a boss has to get a message in front of you.

Wave 1: The first wave of attack comes through the more professional channels like email and your internal work messaging system (Slack, Teams etc.). These are the easiest to achieve plausible deniability. Consequently Wave 1 is straightforward to brush off and plead ignorance of.

Wave 2: The second wave encompasses 'the absolutely-not-professional-channels-but-a-lot-of-bosses-seem-to-think-that-they-are' channels. These include personal texts and WhatsApps. WhatsApp in particular, is the modus operandi for impatient bosses who think annual leave is something that employees take just to ruin their day.

Wave 3: The third wave starts to get into the intrusive territory of social media platforms. And I am not just talking about the big hitters. Name a social media platform and I will show you a story of someone using it to badger someone on holiday. One in particular stays fresh in my mind: a boss decided to set up a Snapchat account just to message one of his younger employees. This would have been an idea, in a complete douchey kind of way, but sadly the said employee didn't have Snapchat, and so the boss ended up following a random person by mistake who, in keeping with internet trolling traditions, promptly pretended to be the employee anyway and caused absolute chaos for the next couple of days. But I digress. The problem with social media is that they are designed to make it very clear that someone is trying to get in contact with you and everyone is fully aware of this. From read receipts, to stating that you are online, to the time stamps of when you yourself might have posted, it's very easy to tell when you were last on your phone. And so, it takes away the main defence of plausible deniability of 'I didn't realise you were trying to get hold of me'.

And I know you can say, 'Oh, but you can just block them.' But this isn't some internet troll sending you messages about why 5G is trying to kill you. This is your actual boss who you are going to have to face next Monday.

Wave 4: Finally, you come to the fourth wave of attack. And it is here we start to plumb the real depths of internet potential with strategies that are equal parts creepy and creative. I use the word 'creative' loosely here simply because I couldn't think of a word that meant 'no one with even the slightest social EQ would ever think this is an acceptable thing to do', rather than any actual admiration for this branch of 'out of the box' thinking.

If I were to pick a couple of finalists from what was an impressively large pool of candidates, in the red corner, I would put the boss who started bidding on his employee's items they had listed on eBay so that he could contact his employee through his 'buyer alias email address'. To this day I have no idea what the end point of his plan was, but at least he got a great looking lamp out of it. This is a better outcome than the boss I have put in the blue corner, who tried to message on Instagram the teenage sister of the employee who was on holiday in order to ask her to pass on a message. HR was notified and the boss promptly found himself on his very own holiday, one without an end date. As a rule of thumb, if you find yourself grooming teenagers on the internet in any capacity then you have strayed outside what can be broadly considered your 'management remit'.

So what can you do? That is the question. I know it is tempting to just say 'well, this is my holiday and they can do one' and I am completely on your side. Of course, that is what you should be allowed to do. There are a lot of amazing managers and business owners who completely respect annual leave and would never do anything close to resembling this. The challenge is that the type of boss who is going to try and hack your eBay bids. And because they are not one of the good ones, they are going to respond to any attempts to ignore them with a complete lack of rationality. And so, people who either are genuinely scared or just can't be bothered to deal with the grief that they would face if they did ignore them, inevitably get dragged into doing work.

We are going to look at how we can prevent this from happening to you, however I thought it would be worth explaining the context of why bosses are doing this in the first place. It is not, despite popular opinion, because they are hellbent on ruining every scrap of happiness in your life. Most bosses genuinely do want you to have a decent break and have a nice holiday.

The reality is running a business is hard. A lot of company owners, especially those running a small to medium business, do not make much money and are often on the cusp of real financial difficulty. That stress of your entire livelihood being on the line, the pressure of paying salaries each month, being one client loss away from ruin and the loneliness of being isolated from anyone else, really does take a mental toll on you.

You would think larger companies have more power and leeway to issue better policies around communication during annual leave. The reality is that they just don't. Most of these companies are backed by venture capitalists and, speaking as someone who has had appalling experience with VCs in the past, they can make life a living hell for a founder and a business owner.

I say this not to excuse any of the poor behaviour that happens off the back of these pressures, but to provide context as to why so much boss behaviour feels so erratic and stress-fuelled. It is often stress that has simply been put on them and they are passing it down.

With that in mind, let's talk about two solutions: how you can prevent this from happening in the first place and what you should do when this happens to you.

How to prevent this from happening in the first place

I have put together a checklist of six things you can do to help prevent this from happening to you. I know your boss contacting you over your holiday is not your fault, but you are going to be the one who deals with the fallout of this, so we might as well focus on what you can do to at least go some way to mitigating it.

1. Handover

I know handovers, on the day you are leaving for a holiday, can feel about as appealing as explaining how Bitcoin works to your grandad, but I promise you that spending that extra hour can make all the difference to whether you get the break you desperately crave. Write everything up that may or may not come in, and make sure you include two details against each task. The first is a clear deadline for when something needs to be done, the second is to tag everyone who you need to handle this in your absence. Prepare a document that people can refer to and also then copy it again into the body of an email as, for some reason, there are a few people in every organisation who treat email attachments with the same level of caution as authorities do when they find unexploded bombs from the Second World War.

2. Giving people a heads-up

Most of the pressure that comes on holiday comes from external sources. Customers, clients, patrons . . . wherever your business gets its money from, you can guarantee that a disruption to any sort of revenue stream is the quickest way to mess up your time off. Very few bosses message about something that is non-commercial. Don't believe me? When was the last time someone messaged you on holiday to make sure that the company social was still being planned or a worry that someone hadn't received a pay review? A potential income loss? All bets are off I am afraid. What you can do personally to counter this, is to message the people who might cause that disruption. If you are client-facing, give them a heads-up and let them know who they can contact while you are away. If you run an e-commerce business, make sure everyone knows the protocols if something goes down. You can't prepare for everything, but hopefully you can at least cover the obvious potential issues.

3. Out of Office

If you fail with this, then you are going on the blame sheet I'm afraid. Do not forget to put an Out of Office on and to treat it like an incredibly important part of going away. Too often, people treat it with as much care and attention as your dad does the rental car on the family holiday. 'I am off on holiday' simply isn't going to work for this. Make sure you are specific about how long you are going to be away for and to make it clear who the person should reach out to in your absence. It is worth putting it on a few hours before you finally clock off as sometimes emails or messages arrive just before you leave, and things get missed.

4. Remind your boss personally

It is frustrating to have to hold the hand of someone who is supposedly more senior and is almost certainly better paid. But I remind you again that if you don't do this, then the only person who is going to be impacted is you. It is in your best interests to make sure they have as little excuse as possible to get in touch with you. Put some time in the diary with them to remind them! The purpose of this meeting is twofold. The first is to remind them that you are going away in the first place. You will be honestly astounded how often bosses just don't clock when their team are away and so are completely unprepared. And it is that unpreparedness that is usually the trigger to getting in touch. Walk them through when you are away and who the best person they should go to in your absence is.

The second purpose of the meeting is to go to great lengths about how you are 'going to be checking in' (don't worry, you don't have to) but you are going away to a place with very limited signal and that you will likely not have access during the day. This might give them pause when it comes to getting hold of you and also sets you up nicely for what you can actually do if they do reach out. The obvious counter is that some bosses may either reject or ignore the invite for a meeting. If that happens, message them directly explaining what the meeting is for and, as a last resort, drop them a detailed email directly reminding them that you are off and what they may need from you.

5. Work phone

I know that some companies are unbelievably cheap, but it is worth asking if you can get a work phone. There are a variety of reasons you can give to why you should get one. You need access to additional social media accounts, the amount of client calls that you do, or even as a cost saver to avoid companies having to pay your phone bill. It is worth the conversation. Yes, it is a faff charging two phones and having two numbers, but it is the single easiest way to disconnect when on holiday. All you do is leave your work mobile on your desk when you head off and try to make sure as few people have your personal number as possible.

6. Glassdoor

Finally, never underestimate how much bosses and managers care about what their Glassdoor account—the anonymous companies ratings website—says and how you can use that to make changes internally. People often forget that you are allowed to leave a review while you are still at the company and it can be a great way to make the business address the problems without having to bear the brunt of any ire that may come from raising it with HR or with the boss directly. This is especially powerful if you can get a couple of other people who have also encountered the issue because it is even more likely to be prioritised. All you have to do is login to Glassdoor and leave an anonymous poor review on their approach to annual leave. I promise you that someone will absolutely pick this up and focus on it. I have seen companies with revenue in the hundreds of millions spend entire board meetings obsessing over Glassdoor reviews, so use it! Make sure you stay anonymous. Don't do it immediately after a big argument with your boss or on a day they know you are on annual leave and be as specific as possible without them being able to directly identify you. There is nothing illegal about leaving a review, but sadly the Venn diagram of 'vindictive bosses' and 'bosses who deserve to have a poor Glassdoor review written about them' overlap with depressing consistency.

What can you do if you are contacted when you are on holiday?

So here is what I have found to be the most effective thing that you can do. Firstly, set your privacy in WhatsApp so people can't see when you were last online. If your boss does text, wait a few hours until you are at the end of the day, then send a very quick message saying you are out with limited signal, but you will try and take a look later. You will be amazed how many problems get solved in the workplace in the time between, a) responding in the first place and, b) being able to look at it properly later. More often than not, the boss will have found someone else to answer the query for you. You, however, have given the pretence of doing your best to help out. Remember our old friend plausible deniability? This line has it in spades and should give you enough coverage. Do not be afraid to just keep using that line. Wait a few hours and then buy yourself more time. Rinse and repeat. For the whole holiday if you have to. Finally, I am hoping this is obvious, but if this continues to happen then I highly recommend that you find a new role. I know this isn't always easy and some people will struggle to move job due to personal circumstances, but this is not someone that you want to be working for in the long run.

If people are constantly on duty in some capacity and not getting a proper chance to switch off, they are going to start suffering. This then starts to impact the business. If more of the team is run down or struggling, efficiencies start to drop, with a knock-on effect on productivity. But it runs deeper than that and feeds cultural problems as well. Guilt and shame are becoming far too common when it comes to people either 'checking in' while on holiday or not even taking the holiday in the first place. This is not benefiting anyone long-term. Annual leave is something that is truly needed. And if someone is directly preventing you from taking it, then I would use that well-earned holiday to think about your next career move. We all work hard, and those weeks off are beyond important, a chance to switch off, relax and recharge your work batteries.

MANAGEMENT STYLES

Employee: Hi Carl, I've just seen that I don't have any shifts next week. Can I ask what's going on?

Employee: Hey Carl, not sure if you saw my last message, but I wanted to check if there was any news?

Employee: Hey Carl, Liam mentioned that this might be about me being late the other week? I know you think that's disrespectful but I did stay late to make up for it, and I am sorry, it won't happen again. If you are annoyed please let me know and we can talk about it.

Employee: Hello?

Considering just how many stories have been shared with me online, you are probably expecting my socials to be the source of the 'worst boss ever' story, but the worst manager I've ever encountered was someone I knew while running my first company.

At the time, this person was a client who ran a large business in London, and because of the size of the business, they had a lot of staff and I have never seen such a spectacular mess of a team. They are the real Patient Zero of the worst boss series. Maybe I should send them a card.

The reason he stuck in my mind so clearly is not because of his personality, but how he went about trying to get things done. Don't get me wrong, he was incredibly tedious to deal with. He was a coward, incredibly belittling of junior team members while being sickly sweet with people more senior which would have been bad enough, but he paired this charming personality with a deliberate strategy around management that was so moronic he has to be given the crown and top spot.

So how did he achieve such an honour? Well, he started off by buying a book on management. I would like to firmly put on the record that this was not the bit I objected to, for obvious reasons. This particular book was about different management styles and the premise was that you would read about the various types of managers and this would help guide you towards the style that best suited your personality, and give you a breakdown of what the pros and cons for each style was. However, (and I stress again that this was deliberate because he thought it was a great idea) he decided that what he would do is simply rotate management styles each week. Meaning one week he would take on the role of an authoritative boss, the next week a supporting one, etc. What was worse, he didn't tell his team this at all, and so, from their perspective they ended up with a Jekyll and Hyde situation where they simply had no idea how to handle or work with him.

I know this might not sound as bad as, for example, the boss who threw a hissy fit because his team didn't buy him a Christmas present, but the reason it is number one in my mind is for three reasons: firstly, this was a deliberate move that he genuinely thought was a good idea; secondly, even if he was a combination of the finest motivator and inspirational leader that humanity had ever seen, he would not have been able to pull this off simply because being consistent is one of the most important traits in a management role; and, thirdly, I personally spoke to most of his team and I had never seen a team more unmotivated or fed up. Tears and arguments were a daily occurrence, three people had mental breakdowns and were forced to be signed off sick and 65 per cent of the team had quit within 12 months of him adopting this approach. Backstabbing, jealousy, even actual fights. All it was missing was locusts outside the window and four horsemen trotting into reception. It was the single biggest backfire of a management approach I have ever witnessed. It was just diabolical from start to finish.

I then found out that the reason such chaos had been allowed to reign for so long, without anyone on the board or HQ stepping in, was because they too were going through a spectacular series of events themselves. One of them had been having an affair with a junior team member whom he had promoted to the board and that had led to him being fired when it had come out. These were not competent people.

The main problem in taking on this particular 'strategy', and please read that word in the most sarcastic voice you can, is that he broke one of the biggest and most important management rules, specifically the need to be consistent.

Being consistent and having a specific management style is so important to bring stability to a team. For teams to thrive and grow they need to feel secure and the only way that they can do so is to know where they are at with their manager or boss. It's been reported by McKinsey that 86 per cent of your happiness at work is tied directly to your manager or boss. That means that even if you work for the worst company in the world but have an amazing boss, you are more likely to be happy than if you work at your dream company but under someone who you find intolerable.

It goes even further. Who you work directly for is so important that they can have the same impact on your mental health as your spouse or partner; a study showed that 69 per cent of people said that their bad boss does just as much damage as an unhappy relationship.

All of which brings us to the topic of management training. Or, more specifically, the lack of it. Research unequivocally shows that the better the management in the business, the higher the growth and revenue. There is also the absolutely undeniable fact that the single biggest reason why people leave a business is directly linked to who is managing them.

With such huge upsides to getting it right and significant downsides to cocking it up, it is remarkable when I tell you that 42 per cent of all managers do not believe that the company has set them up to succeed. In fact, to take it a step further, only 20 per cent of managers think companies have given them the required level of training needed to do a good job.

I do think this is important to remember. One of the key points of this book is that most 'bad bosses' are coming from a place of ignorance or incompetence rather than deliberately going out of their way to make your life miserable. While that doesn't do you much good when you are in the depths of an awful situation, it does give me hope that this is a problem we could fix.

Some will argue that there is little management training because it relies mostly on soft skills and they are nearly always neglected within businesses, but I disagree with that. Sales and client services are also reliant on soft skills, and yet companies will throw thousands at even the slightest increase there.

I remember a very funny, albeit slightly depressing, story from an HR Manager who got in touch with me. This person worked at a company that claimed they had a phenomenal training budget for managers to use to train their team. They apparently had run a cost analysis on said training budget and found out that some of the things that they spent more on than said management training included, but was not limited to, flowers for their reception, snacks for the kitchen and, inexplicably, a magician for the Christmas party. I was assured he was a very good magician but he was sadly overshadowed by the actual staff as it turned out they had their own disappearing trick as people quit in droves.

Stability doesn't guarantee a good boss sadly. It turns out people seem to be very capable of consistently being an arsehole at work – but it does allow you to start to understand how to manage your boss. Understanding what type of management style they have not only gives you an insight into what aspect of their management you might be able to have an impact on but, more importantly, it will help you mitigate the damage when it comes to their worst habits.

That, then, is the focus of this chapter: the different types of management styles and specifically those to look out for and avoid in your career.

It is important to understand that you rarely find a universal bad boss. Everyone is different and some things that might be a complete deal breaker for you may not affect someone else as badly.

Take micromanagement as a style for example. This is one of the most unpopular types of management, but people have different levels of what they are willing to accept. Some people require a more hands-on management approach and need more reassurance than someone who doesn't need anything more than a small check-in once a week.

I remember one story about a boss where half her team couldn't stand her, and the other half thought she was absolutely brilliant. It turned out that anyone who worked remotely thought she was fantastic but anyone who was in the office with her found her much too much. She just couldn't help but get involved.

All of these factors are worth bearing in mind as we go through what I think are the worst types of management styles that you can come across and how to identify that you have one of these bosses.

Bad management styles

THE NEPOTISM BOSS

This particular boss will surround themselves with a clique and will always promote their friends or, if you are feeling harsh, sycophants, above the best candidate. They also tend to be incredibly insular in how they run the team or company.

Outside of a small group of cronies, they will not trust others at all, leading to a breakdown in communication. They will very likely have a nickname for said small group of cronies as well, which you can confidently assume will be an obnoxious choice.

The worst example I saw of this was a recruitment company where the founder had a few colleagues who were senior management and they couldn't have had less of a clue of the damage they were doing to their business. They called themselves 'The Wolf Pack' (of course they did) and their approach to promotions was to have an evening once a quarter where anyone who wanted to put themselves forward for a promotion would be invited to present their reasoning to the 'wolf pack', who would drink and vote on whether they thought they deserved it. It made some of the hazing stories from American colleges look tame.

So how can we mitigate this type of management style? The nepotism boss will be quick to criticise much more than other managers, and so ensuring the work is done to the required style is key, and keeping your boss in the loop as to results is absolutely essential because it avoids someone else being given credit for it. I am not saying you need to send emails titled 'Look how amazing I am' but recognition emails designed as status updates are easy to do and have the added benefit of documenting everything in the long run.

Alongside this, spending additional time building rapport with your colleagues and co-workers is a really beneficial approach to dealing with this type of management as well. It helps avoid the team being divided and ensures there is more transparency and respect to help draw away from the more toxic element of favouritism.

THE INCOMPETENT BOSS

This is one of the weirder bosses on the list, because more than likely, this boss is a delightful person. Affable, mild-mannered, easy to chat to and someone you can get on with.

The challenge is that they are just incredibly bad at their job and simply not able to deliver on the actual core responsibilities.

Now I know the temptation is to simply think that bosses get in the way anyway and having someone who is useless is a lot better than someone who gets too involved, but the reality is that if you have someone at the top not pulling their weight, the work-load that they should be doing doesn't just disappear.

Instead, it inevitably heads downwards, resulting in people more junior to the boss having to pick up the slack. And they often do so without additional pay or credit.

The other key factor is that this type of boss will tend to be over-lenient. Again, this sounds a lot better than it is. There are so many examples of bosses being overzealous with the rules; in fact, I remember one boss who, whenever he saw his team yawning at their desk, would take them outside to tell them off. Can you imagine a bigger waste of time? And so, if you have been on the receiving end of this, I totally understand why someone who lets things go is a tempting option for a boss. But a team needs some-one to tell them when they are doing something wrong.

Whether it deals with attitude or deliverables the boss's job is to get the best out of the team, and you cannot do that if no one ever gets told they are doing something wrong. A workplace like that very quickly leads to similar challenges provided by teenagers who have never once been told off by their parents, and I think we all know enough examples of that to understand what I am talking about here.

The importance of documenting when you have an incompetent boss cannot be overemphasised. Keeping track and having a paper trail will not only ensure that the boss doesn't forget but it can also cover for you when things go especially wrong under the boss's leadership and people are looking for accountability.

Alongside this, having an 'ask for forgiveness rather than permission' attitude is a sensible approach as you can get a lot of things done before it can go wrong, helping to limit the damage done.

Finally, ensuring communication with the boss is key. Do not try to cut them out, instead focus on being as proactive as possible and keeping them as up-to-date as you can, again keeping everyone on the same page.

THE INFLEXIBLE BOSS

You think your dad is stubborn about politics, you have not seen the half of it. This is the type of boss where, once a decision has been made, nothing will change their mind. You can have every expert in the world walk into their office and tell them that they have made the wrong call, but they will simply dig their heels in and refuse to budge.

This boss is rarely angry, their attitude tends to be a little bit colder and more aloof, but the core problem of being incapable of being wrong and changing their mind creates a phenomenally difficult work environment simply because things change when running a business. What makes sense one day may not be the slam dunk it once was.

The other key characteristic of this type of boss is they never involve you in their decision-making, and so the working relationship can often feel quite parental with them just telling you what to do rather than feeling like you have arrived at the decision together.

Finally, woe betide trying to get this boss to embrace anything even remotely new from a technological perspective. And when I say new, I am not talking about cutting-edge AI tools, I am talking about the actual basics such as email and having a smartphone. I know of one boss who still refuses to use email, and instead would simply dictate to his assistant who would dutifully write up his emails for him.

The trick to handle this situation is to heavily rely on data and numbers. This is not the type of boss that is going to be swayed by any emotive pleading, and so evidence is your best chance to get anything over the line. Keep the emotion out of it and focus on the outcome or advantages of why you are requesting change in the first place.

The other method is to adopt a more gradual approach to disruption. Allow the boss to become accustomed to tweaks over time. This requires more of a lead time, so factor that into your schedule, but making changes slower and in a more gradual way, while taking longer, will have a much bigger chance of being signed off.

THE EGOTISTICAL BOSS

The best way that I can describe the egotistical boss is to compare them to a populist political leader. They are big fans of the stage; they will be very quick to steal credit and glory and will be equally quick to throw someone else in front of the bus to take the fall for a mistake they have made.

There is a falseness to this particular type of boss, making them incredibly hard to trust. It is a trait a lot of founders struggle with. They typically try to make the company about them rather than focusing on building the actual brand of the business.

At their best, they can make you feel incredibly important and a key cornerstone of the organisation, at their worst, there is a real sliminess to their characters and they will tell you whatever they think you want to hear in order for them to get through the conversation that you are having with them.

It goes without saying that these types of bosses will be all over LinkedIn and will likely have a podcast where they discuss topics they know very little about, but with the confidence of someone who is used to blustering their way through conversations.

Yes, before anyone points it out, I am fully aware that I tick all of those requirements as well . . .

This type of boss can in fact be a relatively easy boss to handle, though you can feel a bit grimy doing it. In short, you need to acknowledge their strengths and to align your ideas and what you want with their vision. When interacting with them, letting them talk is key but it is important that you focus on results and give the impression that it was thanks to the boss that you were able to achieve such impressive numbers or targets.

THE IRATE BOSS

I would say this boss is the closest to the cliché of the 'bad boss'. This is the in-your-face, screaming and bellowing boss that dominates cartoons and, sadly, a lot of my stories on social media.

The main problem I have with this type of boss is that they will nearly always have a quick fuse and have a nasty tendency to lash out every time something upsets them which will often result in calling out employees in public.

What is worse is that they will often try to justify the behaviour by trying to claim that it is a strategic use of anger to motivate their team rather than just ill-discipline and an inability to get over themselves.

The ironic side to this boss is that when they are in a good mood, they can often create some of the best working environments around. Irate bosses will often be inspirational and charismatic and will really be able to ensure their team deliver their potential. But there is always that edge, that feeling of walking on eggshells, where the team knows that they are just one email or call away from having their day ruined.

The inconsistency is particularly annoying to deal with; this boss can take on the chin business-changing news without blinking but then, the next day, the tiniest, most unimportant update can make them lose the plot. I remember one story where the boss punched the wall because the delivery of the plants for the office was delayed by a further week. The fact that the plants were part of a wider effort to make the office feel a bit more zen and relaxing was an irony that was not lost on the person who shared that particular story with me.

When it comes to handling this type of boss, let's make something very clear, nothing is worth being bellowed at. Very few people can handle that type of situation in a way that truly doesn't bother them and so I would always say step one is to look for a new job.

However, if you are in a position where that isn't possible, the trick is to avoid having any sort of discussion or meaningful conversation while they are annoyed and wait for them to calm down. Quick to anger often means quick to calm down, and so I would just do whatever it takes to avoid talking until this happens, when you can have a more rational chat.

Equally as important, is that you don't fight fire with fire. Do not start hitting back with your own temper as much as it might be justified; remember this is about the best outcome for you and it is just a simple fact that shouting at your boss will only hurt you in the long run, as unfair as that might be.

THE PASSIVE-AGGRESSIVE BOSS

I don't know why, but the passive-aggressive boss is up there with the egotistical boss when it comes to the type I dislike the most. There is something about this type in particular that gets under my skin.

Lashing out in anger is never the right thing to do and I am not going to pretend it is, but that comes from a loss of temper which I can understand, if not condone. But there is a real vindictive streak to the way that passive-aggressive bosses act that makes them particularly dislikeable. I think it is because there is an element of revenge to their thinking. You have annoyed or upset them but they are too cowardly to take that head-on and instead resort to underhand *Mean Girls*-style tactics that, considering the power dynamic between boss and employee, I just find pathetic.

One of the absolute classic signs that you are dealing with this type is how they treat someone who has handed in their resignation and working their notice. Any decent boss would recognise the importance and decency of finishing the relationship in as positive a way as possible, but the amount who turn into petty children is ridiculous.

One of the worst stories I have ever heard that genuinely broke my heart a little, was the woman who told me about how, upon handing in her notice, her boss had thrown a leaving party in her name but didn't allow her to attend. Rather than being a celebration and farewell to her, it was a celebration of the fact they wouldn't have to talk to her again. Like I said, pathetic.

The first piece of advice I have for someone who is dealing with a manager like this is not to descend to their level. As tempting as it might be, you will gain nothing from throwing back comments of your own. I know this might be frustrating to hear but I really want to stress how important this piece of advice is.

In fact, the best way to handle someone like this is to make them look their own comments in the eye through the use of clarification. Ask lots of questions, play dumb and pretend you don't notice the passive aggression and kill them with kindness. Bosses who tend to deploy this type of behaviour are ones who hate conflict and will avoid it at all costs and so if you kill them with kindness, but not shy away from asking as many questions as is needed until what they want from you is clear, you may be surprised how quickly this type of behaviour stops.

This is another boss where documenting meetings and promises is important, as this type of character will have no qualms about bailing on a promise or gaslighting you to think you haven't done enough to hit targets.

THE UNETHICAL BOSS

We all have that family member who plays a little bit fast and loose with 'doing the right thing'. One of the many challenges of Covid was that during the restrictions we all found out that we had more of those family members than we realised.

An unethical boss is the person who will frequently test the boundaries of what you might think is, let's say, poor behaviour. To be clear, I am not talking about criminal bosses, or managers that break the law. I am kind of hoping it goes without saying that they should automatically be on this list.

I am talking more along the line of ethics. The boss who will frequently make you feel uncomfortable with how they run the business. It could be the ease with which they lie to staff and clients and ask you to do the same. It could be the way they over-charge customers or try to underpay suppliers.

In short, it will be a constant stream of small things that can add up to pretty big problems in how you feel about yourself and the work that you do. The successful unethical bosses will usually have just enough charm to get away with most of this but it will leave a nagging feeling in the back of your mind that what you are doing is not OK.

If you find yourself in this situation, my honest advice is to find a new role. Nothing is worth feeling bad about yourself and what you do, and if you have a boss like this there is absolutely zero chance that they will change.

THE UNSUPPORTIVE BOSS

Axolotls are a type of amphibian that I had never heard of. I would try and describe them to you but my editor is quite strict on my word count for this book so I am going to save myself a thousand words and just tell you to google it. I highly encourage you to look at them because they are weirdly cute and cheerful looking for amphibians.

The reason they are being mentioned is because they apparently are the worst parents in the animal kingdom. They simply lay their eggs and then bugger off and leave their young to get on with it.

This is not an unfair comparison to an unsupportive boss. That person who simply shows you to your desk and then leaves you to completely and utterly flounder with no support.

A good manager or boss should always be training you and giving you a chance to show what you can do; it is how we all learn. They need to give you the instructions on how to do the role, otherwise you are just aimlessly putting random pieces together with no idea if you are doing it right.

This particular boss weirdly seems to think that this considerable weakness is in fact a strength. 'I like to leave the team to get on with it' or 'I believe in making them jump in at the deep end'. But if the team is just sinking then this approach isn't going to help anyone.

I think the worst trait of this particular boss is when things are going badly they don't step in to shield their team. Whether it is a rude client or someone high up in the business throwing their weight around, the best bosses will shield you or, at the very least, back you up when things are tough. But too often bosses in this category will fall short.

The final characteristic to keep an eye on is a complete lack of career development. They will frequently move or cancel catch-up meetings, be close-mouthed about any potential pay rises or promotions and in general give off a vibe of not being particularly bothered about whether you succeed or not.

In regards to what you do to handle this particular barrel of laughs, the key is to be proactive in requesting as clearly as possible the type of support you need to give your boss the best chance to understand and step up.

The other thing I always recommend in this situation is to seek guidance or an unofficial mentorship from other senior figures or leaders in the business. It's important not to do it in a way that sounds like you are implying your boss is hopeless, but phrasing it in a way that you are just looking to benefit from other people's experience can be a really nice way to mitigate the absence of your existing boss.

The idea of getting additional support extends to your network outside the company as much as possible. Set yourself the goal to try and meet a few more people in your space to have someone you can lean on for ad hoc advice and support. It is something I have done throughout my career.

What can you do?

The above is not an exhaustive list of bad bosses you might be unfortunate enough to cross paths with, but it should give you a good flavour of the variety that you may come across. They all have their strengths and their many, many weaknesses and, because there is so much variety, it is impossible to prepare for everything.

While it would be amazing to get your ideal boss, as I am sure you are aware of by now, that is rarely the case and so it is important to start controlling the areas that you can. The best place to start is identifying how you like to be managed. If you can figure out what type of management works best for you, you can start factoring that into how you approach your work and your career.

1. Identify your motivators

We are all motivated by something. For some of us, it is simply a financial transaction and the size of the paycheck that matters. For others, it is having a healthy work–life balance. Some of us believe passionately in the mission of what we are doing and as long as we have enough to live off then we are happy. Alternatively, you could hate your current role but it is a stepping stone to what you do want to do and so you are happy to suck it up to achieve the end goal.

My point is, we all are motivated by something, and one of the first things to understand about yourself is what gets your juices flowing. This is the time to be honest with yourself. Because if you know what motivates you, you will start to be able to understand, a) what you want to achieve and, b) what you are willing to put up with in order to achieve it.

Produce a list of the things that keep you motivated and get you up in the morning. Then use this list moving forwards to guide every decision you make about your career and your inter-actions with your boss. If your boss is vaguely in the realm of reasonable, I would highly encourage you to tell them what it is that motivates you.

As a boss, I have always found it incredibly helpful when employees say things like 'I really want to get to a point where I am earning this' or some other wider goal; it allows me to shape the strategy of how I interact with them moving forwards in a more productive way. For example, I had one team member who had worked for me for a few years at my first company Verb who said they loved their job but wanted to go travelling and therefore were thinking of handing in their notice.

The average age in the business was about 24 at that time and it didn't take much investigation to find out that a lot of people had this same thought. And so we decided to set up the 'Take Two' initiative where, if you worked two years at the company, you would be allowed to take two months unpaid leave to go travelling. This was great for the team because they were able to tick that off the list with the confidence that they had a job waiting for them when they got back and great for me because I wasn't losing great talent after training them up due to them wanting to go abroad.

2. Assess your working style

There are some bosses that you are never going to be able to work with. However, a lot of management clashes come from simply an incompatibility of personalities rather than incompetence. Understanding the type of people you work best with is an incredibly valuable piece of homework that you can do to try and ensure you end up with someone who you can work well with. As a starting point, there are a bunch of different online personality tests that are available to gauge what type of management style might suit you. Some of these are complete and obvious bullshit and on a par with some of the 'IQ tests' you see knocking around, but some are surprisingly insightful and can give you a good idea as to the type of manager that will work best for you.

However, you can look deeper than this. Try finding a quiet room and do a little self-reflection. How do you like to work? Do you like working with the same three people or like to mix it up? Do you prefer working collaboratively or do you prefer to work on your own? Equally, which parts of the job weigh on your very soul and you absolutely hate? We all have things we relish doing and the parts that we would quite happily never touch again.

For example, I have always hated networking events. I am perfectly happy giving a talk or sitting on a panel, but I am in absolute awe of those who can simply enjoy going into a room of complete strangers to chat. Some people love the social side of work, viewing wining and dining and meeting new people as one of the absolute perks of the job. To those people, I salute you and will happily applaud you doing all of that from the safety of my living room.

My point is that if you don't know what you like, then how is your boss supposed to? Spend some time thinking about this and then try and communicate this to your boss.

3. Reflect on past experiences

Pick up that piece of paper again, or reopen the Word document where you wrote down what it is that motivates you.

I want you to write down when you think you were most happy at work. If you are a glass half-empty sort of person you can approach it as more of a time when you were least miserable.

Now write down the different factors that you think might have contributed to that feeling. Perhaps it was a specific project, a certain person, a work environment that for whatever reason you think made work better for you. It can be as mundane as feeling much better working next to a window or with plants.

It is worth really thinking about this and then going to your manager and saying this to them. I know it feels like your boss should just be good enough to work out what motivates you but this is about what is best for you, and if you have to write down a cheat sheet to make you happy and deliver it to them personally, then it is absolutely in your best interests to do so.

4. Ask your friends and colleagues

It can be tough to be honest with yourself sometimes. It can also be quite tricky when you are right up against the glass to spot the trends and the patterns of what you enjoy and what you don't.

This is not something you have to muscle through on your own. Ask your colleagues, your friends, your family, anyone who knows you well, one simple question, 'how would you manage me if you were my boss?'. I think you would be quite surprised by how accurately they would be able to do so.

In the same way a sibling always knows exactly what to say to get a rise out of you, it turns out that friends are equally good at knowing exactly how best to manage you to do what they want you to. Take from that what you want!

The reality of the situation is that understanding who your manager is and how they go about things is so important when it comes to assessing the best way to approach some of the specifics of the next few chapters such as pay rises and promotions. Taking that time to understand what makes them tick, what their priorities are and where they are going to give you some leeway and where they are going to be strict, is crucial to working out the best way to achieve the goals that you have set for yourself.

6

PAY RISES

Boss: *Hi Debbie, I just wanted to let you know that unfortunately the pay rise you asked for has been rejected.*

Employee: *Hey, that is really frustrating. This is the third time that this has happened. Is there a reason why?*

Boss: *I can't go into the specifics, but I'm confident that you will be successful the next time around. I know the company really values you and all the work you have been doing.*

Employee: *And you know that I have been enjoying it, however I really was sort of banking on this pay rise coming through. My rent has gone up enormously and this is really going to set me back.*

I love this exchange. Not because it was handled well by the boss, it was a car crash from start to finish. No, I love it because it perfectly represents not only just how bad companies and bosses are at having these discussions but also how employees don't help themselves: Debbie also scored an own goal in how she has approached this conversation. And this happens across the board. Whether you are dealing with a start-up with just a few employees or a Fortune 500 company with an HR department, the only consistency I see is just how badly these conversations are all handled.

And the situation is made that much more ridiculous by these same companies sitting around a table and complaining about how much they are paying in recruitment fees hiring people to replace those that have left. The lack of awareness is just incredible. One of the most basic rules of business is that the cheapest way to recruit is to make sure that your team doesn't leave in the first place; ensuring fair and sensible pay rises is the easiest way to cure this problem.

No one is unaware of this. You are hardly going to win a Nobel Prize for pointing out that how much people get paid and how regularly they get a pay rise is tied to the longevity with which they stay at a company. But that still doesn't prevent the issues that Debbie is dealing with materialising for thousands of people every day.

Even when companies do give proper pay rises, they can bungle the messaging. I have been sent a recorded audio of a Zoom call where a very senior director of a top accountancy firm told the group of juniors that they were receiving a 20 per cent raise. A positive piece of news, yes?

Well it would have been, but inexplicably the director then decided to add his two cents saying that he didn't feel like they deserved it at all, but another company had given their juniors a similar raise and so they felt they had to match it and that he thought the whole thing was just pandering.

What followed was one of the biggest mass exodus of graduates the company had ever seen. And this is one of the most successful businesses in the world. Think how bad you have to be at your job as a manager to give someone a 20 per cent raise and still have them leave the meeting annoyed.

The other party trick I have seen employed recently is increasingly creative ways to justify a pay rise that isn't really a pay rise. One company that springs to mind is the one that, instead of giving people an actual increase in the money that they were paid, registered them for a savings course with Ramsey Solutions, the brainchild of the American financial expert Dave Ramsey, stating that, if they followed his advice, it was basically the same as a pay rise. Putting aside how insulting it is to suggest no one knows how to budget, it went down exactly as well as you would expect something as stupid as that would do.

I would understand if there was an underlying financial incentive but as I have mentioned numerous times already throughout this book, people quitting their job is an expensive problem for companies to deal with. Recruiting is one of the biggest costs; from finder fees, training, and often having to hire people at an increased pay to the person who left, these things add up. And so, risking all of that over what is quite a nominal amount for a company is such an unnecessary risk. Most pay rises that people fall out over are often the same price as a boozy director's lunch, and it is a ridiculous thing for a company to risk.

And the reason why people take it so personally when they don't get the pay increase that they were hoping for, is because of the psychological way that it is tied directly to their relationship with their boss.

What I mean by that, is if you have spent a year being told that you are amazing, or praised for how hard you have worked, or been told by your boss how they would be simply lost without you, it makes people feel like they are doing an amazing job and that they are incredibly valued. Of course it does. And so, when that same boss sits down across a table, looks you in the eye and tells you that you aren't getting a pay rise, it can make your entire relationship that has been built over the past year feel completely false. It is the equivalent of going to Paris with your partner who spends the whole journey saying how much they love you and then, instead of the proposal you were expecting, they end up breaking up with you.

And that is the disconnect in a nutshell, because companies treat it like a professional transaction in a professional relationship, but they often forget the human relationship people build with their boss; so they, understandably, respond in the same way they would if anyone who they have a personal relationship with lets them down.

Not that good pay solves everything. There are countless examples of extremely well-paid people who despise their job and the manager they work for. For example, I was recently told a story about a boss who kept taking his employee's car because 'it was a company car and therefore basically his'. He then truly didn't understand why his very well-paid employee was left disgruntled, stranded in the office and not able to get home that evening because his car wasn't where he had left it.

Even money starts to lose its sheen in the face of that sort of behaviour, but people will understandably put up with a lot more if they are truly feeling valued, and the only way to officially validate that feeling is through actions, with a pay rise being the obvious tangible proof of that. Pretty words on their own will only get you so far.

So that is what we will be looking at in this chapter, to try and understand two things: what exactly the main mistakes are and why bosses make them so often; and what the employer and you can do to give yourself the best possible chance.

What do we mean by 'pay rise'?

But we are getting ahead of ourselves. What do I even mean when I say pay rise in this context? I am talking about your annual review. This is where, once a year, people sit down with their boss or manager to discuss how they have done over the past 12 months, discuss the year ahead and, in theory, confirm what pay increase you might be getting.

There is just one big problem.

Companies really don't like giving out pay rises.

While for employees it is one of the most exciting times of the year, for companies it is the complete opposite. Their view is that you are essentially paying more for something you already have. Which kind of makes sense in a frustrating sort of way. If you have ten individuals all doing a job, and you give them a 10 per cent pay rise, your staff costs have gone up by 10 per cent but you are not getting any more value from it. Immediately you have an issue, as employees treat it like one of the most important meetings of the year (which it is), and companies approach it with the same attitude as a teenager does their weekend chores.

Let's begin with the boss at the start of this chapter and his messages to Debbie. One of the most basic rules when it comes to discussing pay is that if you are going to deny someone an increase, then you have got to give them specifics as to why it has been denied, otherwise they will just assume you are being petty for no reason.

The fact that Debbie and him have had multiple pay discussions and she still has no idea why she hasn't received it is inexcusable and the exodus of team members you will have if you adopt this approach cannot be overestimated.

It isn't even that hard. There are two main reasons why you can deny a pay increase: company performance and personal performance. Depending on which one it was, this is what the boss should have said.

Example 1: 'I would love to give you a pay rise, however, unfortunately the company profit margins have dipped below the point at which we are allowed to do so. As soon as they are back in the green, I promise you that I will approve your pay rise and I will give you a monthly update in regards to how the business is doing.'

Example 2: 'The reason we have denied your pay rise is that although we have seen great progress with the way you have handled your clients, we are still seeing that from a time management perspective you aren't quite at the level yet that we need to justify it. For example, the report you turned in late and the client campaign from the other week that was slow to get off the ground. Let's put a meeting in for next quarter and, if we have seen an improvement in that area we will approve the pay rise.'

Now Debbie might not have liked to hear this, or even agree with it, but at least she will understand that there is a method to the madness and that she is being treated like an adult. Instead, the boss offered her nothing but empty platitudes and that is always going to damage the relationship.

The big point to notice about these examples is the use of specifics. One of the best signs that you currently have a good boss is the use of specifics. You can't fake detail. And so, a boss who is across your progress and what is going on in the wider company is able to have those in-depth chats where a lot of the answers lie. If you look at what happened with Debbie, you can just see the lack of detail around timelines or specifics which tells me this boss has not done the basic preparation required to effectively handle this situation.

Not that Debbie necessarily covered herself with glory here. Don't get me wrong, I hold her boss completely responsible and by far and away the guiltiest party here, but 'I want a pay rise because I would like more money' is never going to work.

Everyone would like more money. Even those who don't need more money would still like more money, and so if your plan is to sit down, wring your hands and tell a tale of woe about how expensive everything is, you are not going to get the pay rise that you want. You have to provide a logic to it. I remember I had a team member who said that he wanted a pay rise and, when I asked why, he said that he wanted to buy a second house so he could start letting it out and needed an increase in his salary in order to afford the mortgage. I loved the ambition, but it wasn't exactly the most business savvy response to that question.

In a job interview, if someone asks you why you want the job, answering 'I would like to get paid' is not going to seal the deal for you. It is very much implied, because, let's be honest, you aren't there for the love of the game, but you have to put your best foot forward and justify why you think you are the right fit for the business. Pay discussions are no different.

So how do you prepare for a pay rise meeting?

Let's get back to Debbie. The boss has handled this terribly and has let her down at every conceivable step in the process; so I have nothing but sympathy for her. However, there are areas where Debbie could also have helped herself a little more. You need to approach these meetings as strategically as possible for the best chance at the outcome that you want.

Sometimes you need to view your boss like a toddler. It doesn't matter if they are the ones being difficult, in the end it is going to be you that is impacted, and so it is in your best interests to mitigate it as much as possible.

I have put together a list of four steps to bear in mind for your next pay rise meeting. This is not a guarantee by any means, but it should at the very least help you get closer to what it is you are looking for.

STEP 1: FIND OUT HOW PAY RISES WORK IN YOUR COMPANY

It is OK to make assumptions about some things at work. You can assume that someone will overdo it at the Christmas party.

You can assume that you will end up in an hour's meeting where the same outcome could have been achieved with a one-sentence email. You can assume that it will sometimes feel like one of your clients is deliberately trying to make your life harder than it needs to be.

However, when it comes to pay rises, never, ever assume anything. Do your homework and find out exactly how it works at your company. Does it work on an annual basis? Which month of the year is it? How far in advance do pay rises need to be submitted with the finance team to be approved? Is there a framework or checklist with which salary increases are decided? What is the maximum increase you can get? You need all of these answers in order to give yourself the best possible chance.

Different businesses operate in different ways, but the one thing they all have in common is that they very rarely volunteer this information. In fact, trying to find out these details is like trying to rent a decent property in London; it is technically possible but feels like it has been made deliberately harder than it needs to be.

The best place to start asking about your company's pay rise process is your manager. It can be added onto the end of another meeting, and it can be as casual as 'I just had a few questions around how the company handles pay rises if that's OK.' If they say they don't know, my advice would be to speak to someone from HR. If they don't know, then the final stop will be speaking to the person in charge of finance. It's important to note that if you are working for a small company that doesn't have an HR department, the best person to speak to is one of the directors of the business. I know talking about money can be uncomfortable, especially with people you don't perhaps interact with on a day-to-day basis, but remember these are all completely reasonable questions that they will have likely been asked a number of times. If any company gives you grief about it, then they are truly not worthy of your time. If they're going to get funny about this, imagine what they will be like when it comes to other areas.

There are some genuinely spectacular ways bosses and companies have tried to claim they have given a pay rise without actually having to increase the amount they pay. I remember one boss tried to claim that, because inflation was coming down, people technically had more money and that could count as a pay bump.

Putting aside how alarming it is that this is how someone who runs a company thinks inflation works, it shows why you need to take this so seriously. It is beyond important to have this information because it allows you to pitch your salary increase within the range of what is possible. You don't want to ask for too little and lose out on a bigger pay rise than they would be willing to offer. Equally, you don't want to go too high, and risk being rejected completely. Finding that range out is key to avoiding both.

STEP 2: GIVE YOUR MANAGER A HEADS-UP

A pay discussion should always be face to face rather than an email or message, however it is worth giving your boss a heads-up a couple of weeks ahead of time that you would like to discuss an increase in pay in that meeting.

This prevents a delaying tactic a lot of companies do where they say 'I will review and get back to you.' The reason why you want to avoid that is twofold: it can sometimes take months and delays you getting the increase; and it can sadly often be translated as 'ugh, can't really be bothered with this but will just say that to get through this meeting'. Tinder matches promising to message about a second date are more reliable.

However, if you give them that heads-up with plenty of time that you want to discuss a pay increase, it takes away the option of them saying such things and forces them to find out the relevant information before the meeting, meaning you can have an actual chat about pay at the appropriate time.

STEP 3: DO YOUR RESEARCH

Find out what you are worth and provide evidence that you deserve it. Now the evidence part of this is very important. It doesn't matter how many times L'Oréal tries to convince us otherwise, I am worth it just 'because' is not going to get you anywhere.

It also can't be anecdotal. 'My mate Dave told me in the pub the other day that I should be paid way more' is also not going to have the impact you might think it should. In fact, there are only three resources that you should be pulling on to prove exactly why you should be paid more.

The first is referring to the wider market to establish what people doing the same job as you at other companies are being paid. Glassdoor, competitor websites and job advertisements are good places to get this type of information.

The second is to directly bring up successes that you have had that have benefited the company commercially. Or, to rephrase it in a rather crass way, how much cash did you make last year for the company? It can be both direct and indirect, but being able to say 'I delivered this for the business last year and I am keen to deliver even more this year, however in return I would like to be paid x' is a really great line. And I know it is a good line because I have given several people pay raises for exactly this. It is important to talk about the future as well as the past. Highlight what you have done and then make it clear you are determined to surpass it the following year.

Finally, refer to the job spec of both your current role and the role above you. This is a really good way to justify a pay rise because you are making it clear that if you were to leave, they would likely have to hire someone more senior to you in order to fulfil the same duties due to the tendency of a lot of business owners not to recognise the level at which their employees are working at.

I cannot overstate how important it is you understand that this is not the meeting for humble modesty and sharing credit. This is the time to put yourself forward at every single possible moment. It is something that a lot of people struggle with, however it is so important to channel your inner Instagram influencer and really go out of your way to show off and make it abundantly clear how valuable you are.

STEP 4: ASK FOR MORE THAN YOU WANT

Companies waste a lot of money. That is just a fact. Sometimes they waste it on good ideas that are poorly executed, sometimes they waste it on bad ideas that were never going to work, but someone senior 'just had a good feeling about it'. One boss I knew of kept his tennis coach on retainer, which didn't quite feel like an essential business cost.

The one thing companies do take very seriously though, and this is universal, is negotiating employee pay rises.

Luckily for you, for reasons I have never quite understood, they only seem to have one tactic in regards to how they do it. And it goes like this.

They will never offer you an increase directly. What they will do instead is ask you what you would like and then, no matter what you say, they will always come back with something along the lines of 'we can't offer you that amount, but we can offer you something in the middle'. The reason they do this is because they know a lot of people feel awkward discussing pay and trade off that very fact.

Fortunately, because it is an incredibly childish strategy, there is a very simple way to counter it. You just ask for more than you want. Take the number you would be happy with and add 10–15 per cent on top of that. And then, when they do beat you down to your original number, graciously accept.

I know it can feel silly playing these games, and of course in an ideal world this would be completely unnecessary. Companies should know the value individuals offer and should pay them accordingly. However, this is about the end result, and if you have to say a couple of scripted lines to get what you deserve, then so be it!

The classic mistakes companies make

Which brings us back to the underlying question: what are the mistakes that companies are making and why are they making them so often? I have been sent over 200,000 stories and messages about bad bosses, and issues with pay are at the very top of the list of biggest frustrations. Interestingly, this theme travels across all countries and sectors; making a complete hash of a pay rise discussion is one of the few things that genuinely unites us as a society.

I have compiled all of these stories and categorised them into five of the biggest tell-tale signs that your boss is going about things in the wrong way.

1. NO STRUCTURE OR PROCESS

If a company doesn't have a clear structure or scorecard with which they give out pay rises then, by very definition, they are going to be giving them out inconsistently, and nothing leads to resentment and frustration quicker than people feeling they are being treated unfairly.

The reason for this is that your boss can't really justify the decisions they are making. And you can always spot one of these bosses, because they don't have the data or evidence to back up their decisions. So when you ask them to explain their decision, they will start blustering and throwing out broad motivational quotes that sounds like they are pitching for a job writing fortune cookies.

Alongside this, you will also find the boss who, regardless of the fact they work in a company with established processes, is too disorganised to sort themselves out to give you the best possible chance of getting the result you want. You all know the type, they are the ones who spend their lives talking about how they are 'busy' or 'have a lot on' but you haven't seen them accomplish a task since last Easter.

Let's be very clear, these managers are idiots. All this behaviour will achieve is demotivate their team and often lead to their staff quitting.

However, getting to call them an idiot is of small comfort if you are sitting there having missed out on getting a pay bump.

Whether you are dealing with a disorganised business or a chaotic boss, the solution is the same. You have to take it on and completely own it yourself. For example, instead of leaving it to your boss to arrange the meeting, look at their diary and find an available slot and book it in for them. Think they might be late for the call? Book in an extra half hour in their diary to make sure you have the time to discuss everything. In short, you micromanage the situation in every possible way to make sure that nothing is missed.

And yes, at this point it will feel like you might as well tie their shoelaces for them while you are at it, but remember what we are trying to do here. The goal is to get you paid, not solve the societal problems of idiots being allowed to become managers. There will be plenty of time to complain over a drink once it is done, but if you just sit back and hope for the best you are going to be disappointed.

2. OVERPROMISE AND UNDERDELIVER

Words are easy. Too often we see managers make promises that they either have the full intention of keeping (but things change) or are fully aware that they can't deliver on and are just making a promise to buy themselves some time.

The main problem with making this mistake, is that when a boss promises you money you start to spend it in your head. When it comes round to it and your boss can't deliver, then you end up in a situation where it feels like your manager has taken money off you, rather than denied an increase, which is a huge difference psychologically.

How can you prepare for this if you suspect your boss is all talk? It's simple. Get everything in writing. Every catch-up or one-to-one meeting you have, especially if it pertains to your career or salary, send over an email summarising everything. 'Thanks for the time today, just summarising everything we spoke about . . .' Trust me, in doing so you will help heal a lot of bosses of sudden-onset amnesia.

Getting things in writing will have two main effects. The first is that you will have proof of your conversations, which gives you a lot more power when it comes to holding bosses to their word. The second is that it will start to be a preventative measure. If your manager knows you are going to document what they say every time, they will stop saying things they know aren't true, removing your chances of getting your hopes up.

3. ONLY DISCUSS PAY ONCE A YEAR

For reasons I have never quite understood, managers think that because pay rise and performance conversations typically are scheduled once a year, they should therefore only discuss a pay rise once a year with their team. And then they wonder why there is a gap the size of the Grand Canyon between what they think is fair remuneration and what the employee was hoping for.

There should never be surprises in a pay meeting. There can be disappointment and even annoyance, but if there is a surprise then something has gone very wrong.

As an employee, you should never go into a pay rise meeting with no idea if you are even getting one. If you just assume you are without confirming or asking beforehand, you are leaving yourself open to an enormous blow psychologically. If it is denied, you will again feel like you are losing money rather than simply not getting more (remember the impact a boss overpromising and under-delivering has?) . . .

The best pay rise meeting should just be the rubber stamping of everything you and your manager have agreed upon over the last few weeks, ideally with the setting of the new goals that come with the increase.

What bosses absolutely should not do, yet one of my followers reported that his boss thought this was a 'smart' idea, is tell a member of their team that he would increase their salary by 50 per cent if they achieved their sales target. They worked incredibly hard and achieved that and, instead of paying them what he promised, he lowered that increase to 25 per cent and justified it by saying 'completing your goals should be enough satisfaction'. Now, the infuriating line aside, a 25 per cent pay rise is incredible, but all that employee could see was the loss of the additional 25 per cent rather than the increase.

And of course this should be the manager's responsibility, but you are just as capable of bringing it up beforehand.

4. PAY DISPARITY IN THE TEAM

If you find yourself in a situation where the company you work for spends half the time running around telling everyone that they can't discuss pay and how important it is that you keep it secret, then you can lay even odds that they are undercooking the value of their employees and paying them less than they should.

The reason I know this is because there is genuinely no commercial benefit to keeping salary bands at a company hidden. Having those publicly available and tied to specific job descriptions is such an advantage when managing someone. Literally the only reason they would keep them hidden is because they are either underpaying some of you, or in the case of a company I was speaking to last week, everybody.

Some of the excuses I have heard as to why people are being paid less than they should are beyond pitiful. The most tragic one in my mind was the boss who tried to say that she deliberately paid people different amounts because she knew someone would break their word (and so set it all up as a test to see who she could trust). If you are going to lie, at least try and come up with something vaguely plausible.

So here is my advice. Discuss your pay with your colleagues. Companies will try and imply that this is against the rules, but it is absolutely not and you are free to do so, especially outside of work hours.

But what should you do if you are being paid less than your colleagues? Firstly, and understandably, it feels like such a slap in the face, especially if you contribute more or feel like you are more senior than the person you are being paid less than. It undermines your entire relationship with the boss or company in question, and I do not blame you if you feel like it is something that you won't be able to get over and look to find a new role.

However, if you want to give it a chance first, this is what you should do. Calmly ask your manager about it. Don't come in all guns blazing, that will just put them on the defensive and nothing constructive will happen. Remember, the goal of this is not to make yourself feel better by ranting at your boss, but instead to get your pay up to a fair amount. I know it might feel good to blow off some steam, but keep the long-term goal in mind. I was sent a photo recently where someone, who was quitting their job working in a cinema, instead of just sending an email, decided to go out in style and resign in quite a unique way – as you can see when you scan the QR code below.

Now while that is initially satisfying, and very funny for the rest of us who get to enjoy it, it doesn't exactly help you moving forwards if you adopt this tactic. Instead, ask your manager if it is true, give them a chance to explain and then put forward your argument. The argument needs to be focused on a direct comparison with the person who is paid more than you. Don't get

personal, but instead do a like-for-like comparison with their professional skill set. The three best arguments that you can reach for
are length of service, job title and responsibilities. Any examples
that show why you should be paid equal to, or even above, this
person is a great opportunity to make it absolutely clear why you
are having this conversation.

5. NO TRANSPARENCY AROUND FUTURE EARNINGS

It is perfectly natural for people to be curious as to what their
earning potential is, especially for job roles that are only a couple
of levels in seniority above them.

The simplest way to judge whether a company is paying people
fairly or not is whether they publicly share the salary bands for the
different levels in the company.

Now if they are treating salary bands with the same level
of secrecy you would normally attribute to foreign intelligence
reports, then that is an enormous red flag and you can comfort-
ably put a bet on there being some heavy discrepancies knocking
around the payroll. You quickly get a feel for what someone
with your skills and your seniority can expect to be paid on the
open market. It is absolutely OK to use this information in the
meeting.

All of these mistakes are incredibly easy to fix and I have never
understood why so many companies persist in making them. I
would understand if there was an obvious monetary incentive
that companies can point at and say 'well look, we lost 15 per cent

of our staff because we fucked around with their pay rise but in doing so we doubled profits for the quarter' but they categorically can't. All the numbers say that this will cost the organisation a lot more in the long run.

And so, the final part of this chapter is how I like to approach these processes. Below I have compiled a simple checklist for employers that will solve all of the above problems, and this works across businesses and teams of any size. It just requires some organisation and upfront work. Equally, if you are an employee feel free to share this directly with your manager.

1. Get HR to research what the market rates are for your employees. Please note, these are not what you think they are, or what you hope they are, these need to be what they actually are. Do not be tempted to reduce these. It will cost you in the long run.

2. Do a full assessment of everyone's roles and see if anyone is being underpaid. If they are, address it that very month. If anyone tries to suggest that you should wait until the next pay cycle, politely tell them to go to hell and press on. You have a ticking time bomb on your hands and if you don't get ahead of it, you run the risk of a huge staffing crisis.

3. Establish pay bands for each level of seniority in the company, and make sure there is a job spec against each of those roles so that managers can very easily identify where everyone is at, and justify that position to their team.

4. Split each pay band into three: a junior, mid and senior stage at each job level. This will allow there to be progression at each level in between promotions.

5. Publish the salary bands internally. Everyone should be able to see them. There is no reason why they can't.

6. Make it compulsory for managers to review this on a quarterly basis.

If you follow these simple steps, I promise you that you will reduce staff turnover in your business significantly and your team will be so much happier and more motivated to deliver on the goals of the company.

PROMOTIONS

Employee: *Hi Drew, I just had my review with Susan and she said that I will not be getting the promotion we discussed. I thought we said that if I hit my numbers the job would be mine?*

Boss: *Hi Andy, yes we did say that. But the team and I couldn't help but feel your success was in part due to the Summer promo. With that extra push, we would have expected your numbers to be higher tbh.*

Employee: *That's not what we agreed on.*

Boss: *Sorry you feel that way, but like I said, we really think you could have pushed a little more. Keep doing what you're doing and I'm sure you'll have that promotion in no time.*

Employee: *This is such nonsense.*

Boss: *That's just how it is I'm afraid. Please let's keep this respectful.*

Employee: *Are you joking?*

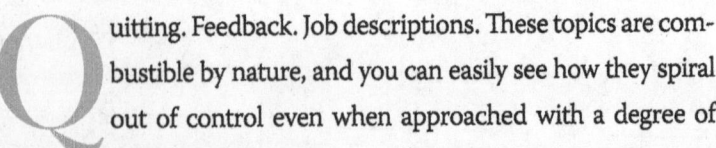

Quitting. Feedback. Job descriptions. These topics are combustible by nature, and you can easily see how they spiral out of control even when approached with a degree of common sense, let alone the sledgehammer approach my DMs are littered with.

But promotions? How is it that what is essentially good news, and a win-win for all involved, can result in as many problems as some of the more toxic issues covered in this book?

And I am not exaggerating when I say this. Promotions are not a pity entry to this book. It is not the coach's son who somehow plays every game despite not being able to tie his own shoelaces, let alone kick the ball. This is a topic that punches far above its weight and more than justifies its inclusion.

The first thing to recognise is that modern society is not as keen on promotions as they might once have been. A poll from Robert Walters recruitment agency about Gen Z in particular, has shown that 69 per cent think that a promotion will be too high pressure and too low a reward to be worth it.

Before we all pile in with the usual comments around snowflakes and avocados, it is worth recognising that Gen Zs are also the most entrepreneurial generation there's ever been, with *Forbes* reporting that 62 per cent have either started or planned to start their own company, and running a business isn't exactly a cakewalk. There is something about working life that is nudging people towards the idea that staying in the same position they are in looks like a much better option than trying to climb the greasy pole of corporate life.

The reality is that most people do want a successful career. Of course they do. If you take a group of graduates and ask them at the start if they want to be successful or not, it is unlikely you will have many in the 'nay' column. And so, in between that bright-eyed and bushy-tailed start and the jaded feeling that promotions aren't worth the aggro, there's something amiss; the numbers are too high for it to be just an isolated group of people.

I'd argue that the biggest issue isn't to do with the promotions themselves, but the way they are either executed or delivered. The truth of the matter is that, as with everything, it is a transactional move. A business has looked at an individual and has estimated that this person, in a position of greater seniority and influence, will produce more revenue than where they currently are, and the additional cost that comes with that promotional salary will be more than mitigated by said additional revenue.

Now, I am aware that is probably the most boring sentence you will ever read when it comes to promotions, and I promise you that we will get to the juicy examples of where people have completely lost the plot with their decision-making, but the reason I have laboured over this is to emphasise the importance of recognising that a promotion is as much for the company or business as it is for the person receiving it. It is a mutually beneficial decision but it is important to recognise that it is the company that takes on the risk as they are the ones paying for the increase.

And so, if companies are getting as much out of it as the employee, it becomes pretty infuriating when bosses act like they are simultaneously bestowing on you the keys to the city and the secret to eternal life. A promotion is a reward, but it is more of a deserved recognition rather than a lottery raffle. You can be grateful of course, but it is a gratitude based on an acknowledgement of everything you have been doing. For bosses to act like a benevolent god bestowing a favour on their unworthy subjects can rankle and sour what should be a genuinely exciting moment.

I remember hearing one story where people who were promoted had to send a thank you card to the Managing Director for said promotion; any hint that you didn't want to do this would be viewed as not caring enough about the company and everything it has done for you. How much of a power trip do you have to be on to think that that is going to have a net benefit to your company? There are Persian emperors from antiquity who expected less recognition than that.

Alongside the terrible delivery, the other core area that causes conflict and issues in the workplace is around the more structural element of how promotions are presented.

One of the more toxic practices that I have seen sneak into companies and teams of late, is the idea of giving someone a promotion without a pay rise. This particular trick is a go-to for a lot of bosses who like to virtue signal that they are a good person, without wanting to do any of the hard work or put their hand into their own pocket.

The good news is that they are easy to spot as they will be the ones with a lot of self-congratulating posts on LinkedIn (photo of them staring intently at a laptop optional, possibly with the Dubai skyline inexplicably in the background) about the importance of valuing your team, while their retention rate lurks in the low 20s. Entrepreneurs and bosses like to do this because it feels like they are giving their team what they want without having to pay them anything extra, therefore costing them nothing.

Promoting without a pay rise is a phenomenon that irritates

me on both a moral level and a commercial one. If your boss tries this, you are not only dealing with someone cheap, but you are also dealing with someone who fundamentally does not understand how to run a team or business. I shouldn't have to tell you that working for an incompetent cheapskate is a red flag, but it is worth writing down just in case!

The reason this particular approach hurts every entrepreneurial bone in my body is that doing this can only lead to two outcomes. Either, you don't have a more senior role, and they have just thrown you the title to shut you up, meaning you will be doing the same role, leading to resentment on your side because you will feel it is not in keeping with your new title. Or, you will be given more responsibility, more duties, a higher proportion of the blame and all the other negatives that come with a promotion without the actual benefit of the higher paycheck, which again will lead to, yep you guessed it, resentment on your side.

That means that this 'clever trick' has a 100 per cent chance of hacking off one of your best employees. Not exactly going to get you into the business hall of fame is it?

The phrase that is used is 'it is on a trial basis'. Often presented with a magnanimous gesture suggesting that your boss is the best person ever to be giving you this chance. Now, I have no issues with trials providing what success looks like at the end is clearly defined and trackable, however you still need to give them the pay rise that comes with that trial. Otherwise, people will rightly quit and the boss will have cost themselves one of their best employees for the sake of the six months of slightly increased salary.

Giving a promotion that isn't really a promotion, whether that is a promotion but no pay rise, or giving the new title when a company doesn't need a more senior role, introduces one of the worst things into a company. Uncertainty. In muddying the water of what the expectations are or what duties you are meant to be performing, it leaves plenty of room for misunderstanding to sneak in, and that is why a huge number of conflicts find their way into my inbox.

One of the more memorable instances of fake promotions that I've seen, was the boss who had three team members who all wanted the same promotion. His solution, and I use that word in the loosest of possible terms, was to give the promotion out with no pay rises, to all three individuals. He then tried to ensure that this stayed a secret by telling all three that they shouldn't say anything to anyone about their promotion 'as he didn't want to upset people'.

My wife says I use the word moron too often when describing people in my work, but I am hoping that even she will give me a pass when talking about this particular genius. Have you ever heard of a plan that was so obviously doomed to fail? Firstly, did he truly think there was a scenario where three people could do the same job without realising? But more importantly, what is the point of a promotion that no one is allowed to know about? The whole purpose is to give people seniority to get things done for the company. Treating it with the secrecy of inducting someone into the Illuminati benefits no one, least of all the boss who is going to, quite rightly, find himself on the wrong side of three pissed off team members.

The final trend I am increasingly seeing is perhaps less toxic than the other examples, but has just as negative an impact: it's the rise of waiting too long before promoting someone. A lot of bosses and managers have in their heads that you need to wait until someone has basically been doing the job already and can tick off all the skills before pulling the trigger. The problem with this is that the 'new' role does not feel fresh and exciting. People do their best work when they are being challenged, and the only way to challenge them is to give them new scenarios and duties to have a crack at.

If the boss waits so long that you have basically already completed the job before you even begin, then things will start to feel jaded pretty quickly and you will find yourself looking for a new opportunity sooner than you might think. Motivation and enjoyment come from the unknown in a job as much as they do from the familiar; if your boss takes that balance away, you will feel the absence.

This is the purpose of this chapter: actively identifying what some of the more toxic practices are so that you can identify which companies you should look to avoid and also recognise if the company you are currently with is handling promotions in a way that can be viewed as healthy. And, because I am doing my absolute best not to completely depress you in this book, I will also walk you through what I think are the signs that a company not only knows what it is doing, but is also one you can trust to have your best interests at heart.

Red flags to watch out for

1. PROMISING PROMOTIONS AND THEN CHANGING THEIR MIND

I thought I would start with the obvious one. This is not a great sign.

Either your boss has done this deliberately, which is an enormous red flag, or they have intended to give you a promotion but have been forced to change their mind; that too is a red flag, because it means you can't have faith in anything they say. I know that last point sounds dramatic, but if you can't trust your boss or leader to do what they promise, then that relationship is a non-starter and you need to get out of there.

As ever with this book, the obvious question you want to ask the boss who does this is 'what happens next?' Because the team will, quite rightly, never believe a word they say, which means they are able to use that move exactly once. That's hardly a reassuring sign when looking for a boss or company to work for in the coming future, let alone the next five years.

2. GIVING OUT PROMOTIONS WITHOUT A PAY RISE

I would argue this is a more recent toxic trait but it is happening more and more. Twenty years ago, the stereotypical bad boss simply wouldn't care enough to give the promotion in the first place. However, with social media documenting their every move, bosses are much more aware that this simply doesn't fly these days. Hence this new trend where they make all the right noises but do everything they can not to make the financial commitment that goes along with it.

What is particularly frustrating, is that this will be presented as a great opportunity for you and your career. While the boss of yesteryear who just flat-out refuses to promote you is a moron – that word again! – there is an honesty to his idiocy that you can respect.

The boss who pretends that he is helping you out, while at the same time refusing to pay you, really is quite hard to like on any level. The fact that they are trying to take credit and validation for doing something that is, a) cheap as hell and, b) genuinely undermining the supposedly 'incredible culture' that they have supposedly spent so much time building, is a tough pill to swallow.

One boss reported to me had given someone three separate promotions without dishing out a single pay rise. At the trajectory she was on, she would have been the first ever CEO who was on the same salary as a junior manager.

The problem with this strategy is that it cheapens promotions within the company. This means that not only will the people receiving them directly feel like they aren't any better off, but they also become distinctly less appealing to the rest of the team whose output may drop when they realise that additional effort doesn't exactly equate to additional pay.

The final point to recognise is that any boss who thinks this is a clever decision, is not a person you can trust. One of the very few perks of being promoted is the pay. Some may think that executives have an easy ride and go from the golf club to the bars without ever doing a hard day's work, and there are of course examples of this, but promotions more often than not come with additional responsibilities, increased targets and additional pressure to deliver even more revenue or growth for the company. Being held responsible for that without the actual pay increase that comes with it doesn't light the motivational fire you would hope a new role would do.

3. PROMISE A PROMOTION IN THE FUTURE

This is the lazy version of promising a promotion and then changing their mind. Don't get me wrong, number one is still despicable, but at least they aren't trying to hide that fact. Like when an internet troll on Twitter/X uses their real name and photo. What they have said and done is still terrible, but you can appreciate that they genuinely believe what they are saying.

This is a lot more cowardly. Promising a promotion in the future but not putting any guarantees or targets in place is incredibly easy. The boss who does this knows it will come back around at some point but is kicking the can down the road. They make it a problem for another day and in the meantime they will get you to work harder for them without any guarantee that it will be rewarded in the way you are expecting.

Any boss who makes these types of promises, but shows a reluctance to deliver by either providing some sort of timescale or requirements in order to achieve said promotion, is almost certainly lying to you. You should view your chance of promotion to be about as likely as someone not using the phrase 'touching base' during a company meeting.

4. PROMOTING THEIR FRIENDS

I remember one of the earliest stories I was ever sent was one of a boss who promoted someone because 'we both play fantasy football'. The justification for this seemed to be based on the idea that as the role required a lot of travelling together, they would have more to talk about.

Putting aside the idea of work journeys where you do nothing but talk about fantasy football, it doesn't sound like a rationale that would feel reassuring if you were part of his team.

In a strange way, I get the inclination for this. The closer you are in rank, the more you talk to them, and so I do understand why promoting someone you feel like you get on with might look like the right move. And, if all other metrics are even, then picking someone whom you think might be able to bring the best out of you isn't the worst approach.

But that is different to just liking someone. You also have the much broader problem of what decisions like this might do to the team morale. Why bother working hard when all you need to do to get ahead is to have a good idea of which players might bring the most success to your fantasy league?

5. MAKING YOU DO THE WORK BUT NOT GIVING YOU THE TITLE

This is the same as number two in this list, but even more dishonest and also somehow stupider. The reason why I emphasise the dishonesty is because this particular gem is nearly always presented to you as your boss doing you a huge favour, rather than the other way around.

By telling you that it is a chance for you to show what you are made of and to prove you have what it takes, they will often conveniently forget to mention the fact that they are getting a senior level of work for a discounted price. In fact, the language is ominously similar to when I hear people try and justify unpaid internships. And if that isn't a red flag, I honestly don't know what is.

6. MOVING TARGETS TO GET PROMOTED

There seems to be an inherent suspicion of anyone who is above or ahead of their target. Often those in power will then look to move the goalposts halfway through.

Beyond the obvious frustration and inevitable drop in motivation if this happens to you, I find the psychology of those managers fascinating. I remember one story where a woman was working incredibly hard and achieved her sales target with two months to spare.

Instead of telling her well done, praising her for her dedication, or anything a normal human with even the vaguest scrap of common sense might do, her boss instead accused her of pretending to be worse at her job than she was; that it was part of some master plan to set her a lower target that she knew she could easily achieve, and that she was giving them no choice but to issue her a new, much higher target. So, did she come back stronger than ever, get her head down and absolutely smash the new target?

No she didn't. She handed in her notice six weeks later. Because of course she did. And if this ever happens to you, you should do the same.

Signs that a company knows what it is doing

I am very aware that this book is supposed to be helping you. I am also aware that me constantly pointing out all of the red flags gives the impression that it is all hopeless. That no matter what you do, you are going to end up working for an absolute cretin who will either not care, be completely incompetent or, like the boss who tried to send his team on a Dave Ramsey savings course in lieu of a pay rise, both.

But that is of course not the case. There are some really incredible companies out there, full of genuinely competent bosses who are a safe pair of hands to trust your career and progression with. And, while the below is not an exhaustive list, I would say these are the indicators that you are looking for to reassure yourself that you are in the right place.

1. SKILL-BASED PROMOTIONS OVER TIME

One of the greenest of green flags that you are looking for in any company is a skill-based approach to promotions. Despite this being by far the fairest and most effective way both to motivate your team and grow your business from a promotions perspective, it is not an approach you see very often.

The main reason for this is that it requires considerably more management time and effort to track. 'Three years at this level and then you get promoted' is much easier to track and manage than identifying a specific level of competency or skill in order to promote your employees.

However, think about how much more motivating it would be if your boss based a promotion on what you can do rather than how long you have done it for. If you knew that the second you reached a certain level, you would receive a pay rise and promotion, you would be so much more motivated to work hard to get to that level quicker, rather than simply 'doing your time' and waiting. And yes, that is an actual prison metaphor which a lot of bosses use when talking about promotions; if that doesn't make my point, I honestly don't know what else does.

Alongside this, if a certain level of skill is required to get a promotion and not a simple time requirement, then it helps solve the problem of people being promoted despite not being qualified or capable of doing the job. The more senior you are, the more damage you can do to the wider team and business, and if people are not capable of doing the work, and simply have been in a certain role for a certain number of years, you are asking for trouble further down the line.

So although the effort to run a company like this is considerably more, the increase a company will see from a revenue and growth perspective is undeniable. Any business that adopts this approach is worth joining.

2. GENUINE TARGETS THAT EVERYONE IS AWARE OF AND CAN TRACK

The whole point of targets is that it takes the subjectivity as to whether someone deserves a promotion or not out of the conversation. Opinions are not a great contribution to those types of decisions, because, by definition, they become something you can disagree with. Whereas facts, despite the evidence of every single Twitter/X thread you have ever come across, are much harder to argue with.

Therefore, what you are looking for when you are planning the next 12–18 months is a list of targets from your boss that you can actively track.

That last bit is key. If you don't know exactly what success looks like, then you need to be proactive in regards to working with your boss to ensure you have a target or goal you both think is challenging but achievable.

Anything vague is just simply not helpful. 'You must increase sales' or 'must keep your clients happy' sounds great but how on earth are you meant to work out if you have done that or not? Increasing your sales by 1 per cent is technically an increase but hardly feels like something that should secure you a promotion. 'Increase your sales by 45 per cent', 'ensure you have a client retention rate of 85 per cent'; those are the types of targets that you are looking for. Any company that invests time to put something like that together is worth their weight in gold and, if there are any managers out there reading this, giving your team legitimate targets like this is one of the easiest ways to motivate them, which can only lead to positive results for your revenue.

3. REJECTING PROMOTIONS

I know that this feels like it is in the wrong list, but one of the healthiest signs of good company culture is a boss who doesn't allow people to be promoted for the sake of it.

Promotions need to be earned. If, as a manager, you have followed number 2 on this list and have agreed targets and the person has missed them, then the correct and best thing you can do is not give them the promotion. It can be a tough conversation, but it gives the message to the business that the boss is fair and reasonable. You're not playing favourites and it sets a standard of success for people to strive for.

If you still don't believe me, have a think back to some of the companies you have worked for. I can almost guarantee there will be someone who springs to mind who you were surprised they even knew how to tie their own shoelaces, let alone fulfil the job requirements they had, inexplicably, been given. I will tell you for free (well free minus the cost of this book) that this will not have been a company where promotions were rejected or, if they were, they were entirely for the wrong reasons.

These 'wrong reasons' are important to mention, just in case anyone misunderstands me and thinks that any boss who rejects any promotion is the new Richard Branson. There are of course some incredibly idiotic and very much incorrect reasons to reject promotions. One of the more memorable ones that I have come across was the boss who decided to promote the least competent person in the team because he wanted to see who was hungry enough to drive them out of the business and take their place, saying 'he is looking for a shark' and for someone who is not afraid to push people out of the way to get what they want.

Leaving aside how unacceptable it is to essentially run a social experiment on your employees like that without their permission, can you imagine promoting someone because you want a person to undermine them so completely that they end up forcing them out of the business and taking their spot? Does that sound like a team in a healthy, revenue-generating sort of mood? What is worse, I didn't even get that one sent in as a story on social media, this boss actually told me in an attempt to prove to me they had a 'high-performance culture'.

The key to this really is having a business that is tough but fair and, most importantly, consistent in the way it handles things. The truth of the matter is that not everyone is ready for promotion, even if they think they are. Promoting someone who isn't ready can cause a huge number of issues within a team. A business that can accurately assess who is ready for that next step and who isn't, is one of the best companies you can work for.

4. REGULAR CHECK-INS

My wife loves watching *Strictly Come Dancing*. And, even though it is not my cup of tea, I have to admit they put on a good show.

The songs, the choreography, the different sets and lighting displays. Genuinely impressive. And they can't fake the building of tension when it comes to the Sunday night show that announces the results of the previous day's performances. The spotlights, the suspense building; they have it down to an art form so that the surprise is as impactful as possible. Excellent television.

Now while tension, uncertainty and the genuine unknown might lead to a great show, if any of these are encroaching on your meetings with your boss, then that is far from ideal. If someone walks into a promotion meeting not knowing if they are going to get it or not, then that boss has already failed.

You should be having regular catch-ups with your boss and, much like discussing salary, promotions should be touched upon regularly. Waiting to have the chat once a year guarantees that you will be miles apart in expectations because you have had over 12 months to drift off the same page with very different results.

Regular catch-ups are an opportunity to talk about how you are getting on, which bits of your job you are doing well, which areas you need to work on, and review targets for your promotion as well as discuss any final bits that you might need. Equally, these meetings can also manage your expectations around why you won't be getting the new title. While that might not feel great to hear at the time, it is a healthy sign that you have a competent boss who is not afraid to have the tough conversations.

One of the biggest reasons why someone might quit over not getting a promotion is because they were unaware there was an area they were falling short in. If your manager has failed to point this out to you then you have no chance to rectify it and you end up being stiffed on a promotion you probably could have easily achieved if you had just been given that piece of feedback.

5. CAREER PATHWAY

A lot of people know what their next job title might be, but how many of you know what the next two or three job titles could look like? If you are lucky enough to have the answers, then you can take quiet satisfaction that you are part of a business that knows how to do it right.

Career pathways are such an easy win for managers. Not only does it show a business has a fundamental grasp of what it takes for employees to feel motivated, but it also shows it is on top of both the current structure of the business as well as how it might need to scale in the future.

Plus, it is such a boost to your career, because knowing what you might be doing in a few years' time can, firstly, allow you to assess if it's what you want to do to begin with and, secondly, it gives you a recipe for what you need to achieve in the next few years.

This in turn boosts the company's numbers, because the team is ambitious and actively developing skills that the company needs in order to thrive. In other words, a complete win-win.

8

FEEDBACK

Boss: Hey James, I just wanted to let you know that while you've been doing a great job over the last few months, we just don't feel you've hit the requirements for us to sign-off your probation. I'll send you over the full details later, but this essentially means we'll be extending your probation for another three months. Have a look through the email later and let me know if you have any questions.

Employee: Hey Sarah, I'm really confused by this. I thought you were happy with my performance? When we caught up at the end of last quarter, you told me things were going well and to keep doing what I'm doing.

Boss: Yes, we're very happy with your attitude and the clients have been loving your work. We just feel like you could do with working on your time management a little more before we sign you off. All of this will be in the email later this evening.

I spend a lot of time in this book talking about communication. I will try and mix it up of course, throwing in a few different words such as 'reporting' or 'meetings', maybe punctuating it with a story or a joke to try and keep you all engaged. But the reality is that communication features in pretty much every chapter. So many of the problems and issues in the workplace are less about people or companies deliberately making your life miserable, and everything to do with good ideas or good intentions being completely bungled in the execution of it all because of poor communication.

That isn't exactly helpful if you are one of those people on the receiving end of such scenarios as it doesn't take away how it feels when it is happening to you, but it is important to recognise that just because someone has made your life hell or a company has completely ruined all motivation you once had, that it is often through incompetence and less than clear communication rather than any sort of nefarious master plan. The good news? It is fixable.

Feedback is the pièce de résistance to this and the absolutely critical pillar of communication. It is the ability of a company or a boss to use praise to ensure people keep doing the bits they are doing well and constructive criticism for areas that can be improved. It is one of the most essential parts of growing a successful company.

And yet, the way that people communicate feedback in practice is often one of the leading causes of team unhappiness and lack of motivation. Whether it is exacerbating existing issues or even turning positive messages sour, it is one of the big challenges in workplaces.

Shouting and shaming

In the spirit of better communication, let's be clear: feedback and shouting are not the same thing. Feedback is a constructive conversation to help you improve. Shouting is just being a moron.

And I've heard some idiotic justification for it; everything from 'it keeps people on their toes' to 'they respect me more for it'. One that really stuck in my mind was from a boss who said that 'it makes me feel better'. That is of course not what we are looking for in a leader at work, someone who will happily ruin everyone else's day just to give themselves momentary relief.

The reality is that if a business has grown with a boss shouting a lot, then it will have done so despite that fact, not thanks to it. Yelling because you are annoyed swiftly loses the 'constructive' part of 'constructive criticism'. There is no benefit; it will just annoy or upset the team so much they either stop working as hard as they were, or even look to move companies. There are not many things that I can say with complete certainty, but I have never, ever, seen or heard of a boss bellowing at someone in a way that helped either them or the company in any way.

The other complete no go area of feedback is public shaming. This is slightly different to just shouting, but there is an amazing correlation between both behaviours. Chances are bosses who do one will also do the other. I heard of a boss who called a team meeting where this poor woman, who had been ill and missed a day, was told that she needed to apologise to every person in the team – literally forced to go around the room, stand in front of every person and apologise for letting them down in some sort of weird ritual. Top tip: if there are any leaders reading this book, if you ever find yourself forcing a team member to do something that could be recognised as a scene from *Game of Thrones*, then you are categorically doing something wrong.

Feedback is crucial to any business and serves three main

purposes for employees. The first is to identify areas where they are doing well and praise them in order to motivate them to keep doing what they are doing. The second is to provide advice and suggestions on areas that they need to improve in. Any boss or manager that is not doing this second part is failing their employee. No one is perfect, and if you are being told by your boss that there is nothing to improve on, it is because your boss is either lazy, unaware or just dodging difficult conversations. That's not a great sign for your future at that particular business.

Thirdly, feedback is an opportunity for employees to raise any worries or concerns. This can be personal or professional, but in short, there should be a safe space for them to raise any problems that might impact their day-to-day role.

The key to unlocking feedback is your catch-up meetings with your manager. Team stand-ups and company meetings all play a part, but for proper feedback to be effective, it needs to be delivered in a safe space to discuss what can be quite tricky topics.

Common mistakes

If you are not having catch-up meetings with your manager, you are going to be struggling. Even if you are, there are a number of red flags to keep an eye out for as a lot of bosses make some truly basic mistakes in how they go about running these meetings.

The first mistake I see is the frequency with which these meetings take place. We all have that friend whom we see once every six months but, when we do, it feels like no time has passed and things are exactly the same. This should not be one of those relationships.

Less is very much not more. You need to be having these chats once every two weeks because otherwise you are allowing too much time and potentially too many issues to build up and be dealt with effectively. The trick to good management is to catch the small things so they don't turn into the big things, and the main weapon in your arsenal to do this is consistency.

I talk about this online a lot and have mentioned it previously in these pages: no one can effectively manage more than five or six people and this is one of the core reasons why. Managing someone requires regular check-ins and if you have too many people as direct reports, the regularity of those sessions is often the first casualty and that turns things into a bloodbath.

The second big mistake I see is the location of these meetings. What you are ideally looking for is a safe space where you feel comfortable enough to raise what can be quite personal problems and issues. Too often managers and leaders will either treat it like a visit from the Royal family, picking the most impressive (read intimidating) location for the meetings or they will have the catch-ups in an area that is way too public that doesn't provide the space people need to open up.

This is a trend that escalates the further up the food chain you go. Having a one-to-one in a boardroom or enormous private office just creates a tension and power dynamic that is so much harder to crack than if you have a more low-key room or even a coffee out of the office. I heard of one boss who had a production team record his one-to-one meetings to share them online to show how good a manager he was. Putting aside how inappropriate that is, can you imagine a scenario where you are less likely to share your concerns or worries? Which is the whole point of the meeting in the first place. Not putting people at ease is guaranteed to make a feedback session go wrong. If a boss makes their employees feel like they are in the Oval Office or the floor of the Roman Senate with dozens of people listening in, then it is not going to help them open up.

But those two mistakes pale in comparison to the big one: a catch-up is not the best time for bosses and managers to discuss general business updates. Not focusing on your employee is the biggest cardinal sin here. Now don't get me wrong, it is necessary to discuss projects and clients, but this meeting is the wrong time to try and do this. The point of a one-to-one is to find out how someone is doing, give them meaningful feedback for them to improve (thus benefiting the company) and also find out if there is anything going wrong. If you are too busy discussing x deadline or y meeting, you are just not going to get to the meat of it all, rendering the whole thing pointless.

Related to this, and another of my personal pet peeves, is the boss who literally can't shut up. A one-to-one has to be a conversation between boss and employee. The whole purpose is for the boss to provide honest feedback in a safe space while also giving the employee a chance to share their thoughts and worries. The idea that it is just an excuse for the manager to monologue their way through it is as frustrating as it is commercially short-sighted. This isn't a soapbox moment, this is a conversation to find out how the employee is doing, and if the employee isn't being given a chance to speak then how can their manager possibly know? If you were dating someone who kept telling you how you were feeling instead of listening to how you actually felt, you would kick them to the kerb pretty damn quickly. Management meetings are no different.

This leads me onto an interesting point. You, the employee, need to play your part in this. This is one of the few occasions where you do get an opportunity to speak your mind. Now, I will heavily caveat that by recognising that some of you may not feel like you have that opportunity. If you don't have proper one-to-ones, or your boss is a megalomaniac or any other scenario where you just feel like you can't give honest feedback, start looking for another job immediately. I mean it, put this book down right now and start updating your CV, because there is no upside to working in an environment like that.

For the rest of you, take ownership of your career. There is no point not telling your boss about any issues or frustrations you have because, odds are, they will likely simply be unaware. Going back to the communication point at the very start of this chapter, most mistakes that I see from bosses and management are based on complete ignorance rather than a deliberate attempt to ruin your career. And so, if you are sitting on something that is actively holding you back and you do not raise it with your boss and just rant about it at the pub after work, then that is as much on you as it is on them.

Textbook feedback fail

Now ordinarily I would provide a list of red flags, and punctuate them with examples of bosses and managers who have done a terrible job implementing everything. However, what I thought I would do here instead is recreate one of the stories that was sent to me via email. It was such a stereotypical example of 'this is the problem with feedback in the workplace' that it was just too good an opportunity not to include it in this chapter. The names are all fictional; the details, sadly, are not.

Luke was late. This would have been annoying on its own, but his message had specifically told me to be in the meeting room by 3.00pm sharp as he only had 20 minutes, so this was particularly frustrating. It didn't help that with a couple of the team out, I was having to plug the gap and you could hear my inbox groaning from half a mile away.

What wasn't helping the situation or my mood was that I wasn't even sure what this meeting was about. Late yesterday Luke had thrown an invite into my diary with the helpfully specific line of 'I need to talk to you, can you book a meeting room for tomorrow?'. He wasn't exactly overloading me with information and had left me with a slightly uneasy feeling all evening, with the added bonus of waking up in the middle of the night in a slight panic as I imagined all the potential ways this meeting could go.

At precisely eleven minutes past three Luke came into the room. Luke had been my boss for a couple of years now. He was approaching 50 and was very much part of the furniture at the company, having been there for close to two decades. He and I weren't particularly close, but we had never had any real issues. He was pretty hands-off as a boss and I was someone who had always just got on with things and so it vaguely worked, and we had never had any big issues. We had also seen a lot of team change over the last six months and I had had to do a lot of onboarding and training up of new team members.

It was weird, that despite knowing this, the message he had sent still slightly had me on edge. If it was good news he would have just told me wouldn't he?

'Sorry I'm late Seb,' Luke said as he sat down.

'No worries. Is everything OK?'

'Yeah of course, I am just aware we missed our last catch-up and thought we should try and squeeze it in now.'

Technically we had missed our last four, but the relief I felt that I wasn't about to be tossed out of the building was such that I wasn't going to start nitpicking.

'Oh right, OK, sure no problem.'

'I wanted to start off with the proposal on Friday, and then we can run through all of the clients just to make sure they are all happy. I have a bit of time tomorrow afternoon so if there are any that you think I should speak to I can do so then.'

It took about ten minutes to run through everything but by the end of it Luke was looking pleased and I was starting to relax.

'Good work, keep me posted on everything.' Luke stood, heading towards the door.

I blinked, slightly taken aback by the abruptness of it all.

'What about me?' I asked.

He turned, looking genuinely surprised that I had spoken. 'What about you?'

'We haven't spoken in a few weeks, is there anything you think I should be focusing on or prioritising?'

'Absolutely not, you are killing it at the moment, keep it going.'

'So nothing that I can do better or should be prioritising?'

'This place would fall apart without you, just keep killing it. Don't know what I would do without you.'

That wasn't as helpful as he seemed to think it was. I knew I had made a couple of mistakes the last few days with everything going on. I opened my mouth to tell him that I was struggling with the workload but before I did Luke glanced at his phone.

'Damn I need to give him a quick call. Give me a shout about how the next couple of days go. I will try and find some time to chat next month.'

This particular story is representative of so many management meetings that happen around the world that it was a no-brainer to include it. Luke didn't shout, he didn't swear, he didn't throw something across the room, he didn't do any of the clichéd, *Devil Wears Prada* things people expect of terrible bosses. That said, he let Seb down at pretty much every single point of the interaction.

First off, if you are a senior leader in a business, never, ever put a meeting in the diary without at least giving some reassurance that it isn't anything serious. People will just assume the worst and they are going to be worried for no reason. But Luke went even further here; by not telling Seb it was their catch-up he gave Seb no chance to prepare any thoughts on his side. Feedback is a two-way conversation and if you ambush someone they are hardly going to be fully prepped and ready to go.

The next bit that I didn't like was how infrequently these meetings are happening. Work diaries fill up, unexpected requirements arrive, meetings get moved – I get it, I have moved my fair share – but it is amazing how important clients manage to stay in the diary and are untouchable and yet one-to-one meetings are moved constantly. It reveals priorities and makes it clear the boss doesn't treat it with the importance that they should.

And you might be able to forgive Luke for all of this if he then conducted an engaging and considerate one-to-one, but even the most bootlicking employee would struggle to make a case for this. He used the time as a quick status meeting asking about specific projects and clients. But this is the opportunity to help the business out as a boss by reinforcing good behaviour and correcting or improving areas that aren't working as well; the fact that so many bosses completely neglect this is beyond frustrating.

The monumental failure of what was a genuinely impressive amount of errors from Luke was when Seb asked him if there was anything else that he could be looking to improve and Luke simply said 'No you are killing it.'

I know that might look like one of the nicer things that a boss might say to you. And indeed, when you stack it up against the boss who told a woman whose very ill father had finally died after a long illness that 'at least you can now focus on your work and stop being distracted', it might look like something that we can let go.

However, this is the one time where you should be telling your team member exactly what they are doing well and areas they can improve. No one is perfect, and it is one of your core duties to train and develop your team, and to simply throw in a casual 'good job buddy' is simply not good enough.

And that brings us nicely to the pinnacle of the complete disaster that was Luke's management approach. How, in all that is holy, in a one-to-one meeting with one of your team which is specifically designed to have an honest chat about how things are going, do you not ask the simple question 'how are you doing?'

Seb was clearly starting to feel a bit overwhelmed from covering the work of the people who were off. What is sad about the whole thing is that if Seb was to quit from burnout in four months' time, Luke is the kind of boss who would go around saying 'it came out of the blue, I had no idea.' Of course you had no idea, you did not ask.

One of the weirdest things I find about bosses who do this is the excuse they nearly always give. 'No one told me you are meant to ask that.' Now I am a huge advocate for management training and think it is something that every company should invest in, but I am sceptical about this excuse. Asking someone how they are doing is very much 'Being a person 101'. There is no other human interaction where you meet someone once every two weeks for a half-hour chat and don't ask how they are doing. The idea that grown adults need to be coached to do this feels like a bit of a cop out and not one that I am going to accept anytime soon.

But that understanding doesn't help you if you are in the same position that Seb is. It feels harsh to say that Seb did anything wrong because in every sense of the word it should be Luke, as the manager, taking the lead, however this book isn't about what is fair, and everything to do with helping you get the outcome you want.

The reality is that Seb could have been a bit more proactive. He could have asked what the meeting was about under the pretence of 'wanting to make sure I have everything you might need ready for the meeting' and he could have asked for more time to talk through the challenges that he is having. It can feel awkward doing so, but forcing your manager to address the things you want to talk about is an important skill to develop because it will benefit you so much in the long run. For example, Seb could have responded to Luke's initial message saying something like 'that sounds good, there are a couple of things that I want to chat through as well' and then gone into the meeting with an agenda. However, in sitting back and hoping Luke would ask (and again, I am not defending that Luke didn't) meant that that opportunity was missed.

Points to watch for

What I thought would be helpful is to finish this chapter off with what I would consider green flags for any one-to-one that you have, while also including the flip side of how these can be conducted badly. If your boss does any of these well, you can be reasonably confident that they know what they are doing and if you are in the boss's shoes one day, this is what you should be emulating!

1. ACTUAL TRAINING AND FEEDBACK

If your boss is not giving you actual constructive criticism which you can go away and work on to improve, then they are failing you. It really is as simple as that. Not least because, more often than not, people have no idea they are making the mistake in the first place.

But in fact, it goes a bit further. A good boss or manager should be helping you come up with a plan to improve. They can't just say 'you are terrible on the phone with clients' and leave you just to flounder your way through it on your own. Firstly, that is one of the quicker ways for someone's motivation to completely drop, and secondly, that is hardly a bedrock for success if the boss is simply leaving you to figure out how to communicate with clients.

What you are looking for is a boss who says something like, 'there are a few elements of how you talk to clients on calls which I think we can work on, so I thought we could do a few calls together so you can get a feel for how I might approach it.'

Another important point to flag at this stage is that there is 'helpfully critical' and then 'overly critical'. A good manager knows to prioritise feedback and give you two or three main areas to focus on, rather than a complete character assassination of every single tiny thing you have done wrong. If you find yourself in a company where it feels like you are being told off for breathing too loudly, then my advice would be to look to move on as soon as you can.

Finally, I can't stress enough how important it is to listen to your boss when they give you criticism. Much like relationships, once you have had a couple of bad bosses it is quite natural to be pretty cynical about any boss telling you where you are going wrong and it is really important to take that moment and think about whether what they are telling you is fair. Not taking feedback seriously will get you nowhere in life.

2. ARE YOU ON TRACK FOR THE YEAR?

Building up feedback for the big reveal at more important meetings such as the annual review is one of the quicker ways to ensure a team's productivity falls off a cliff face. Even if it is bad news, a good boss should be managing your expectations properly throughout the year so as to avoid you feeling completely blindsided when you hear that you aren't on track to getting the promotion or pay raise that you might think you deserve or enjoy. I would go so far as to say that even if you are blindsided by good news, this still isn't a great sign. I am a little more sympathetic because it is obviously a lovely moment to be able to tell someone they are promoted or getting the pay raise that they deserve, but it shouldn't come as a complete bolt from the blue.

One of the best signs you have that a boss or manager is on top of this is that they will proactively bring up areas they think you need to improve, especially if they provide actual training and suggestions of how you might do it better next time. The best managers recognise that it is entirely in their own interest to get their team performing as well as can be and so they will look to bring up things you are doing wrong in a constructive way that gives you the best chance to get it right the next time.

A manager who points out areas you need to improve throughout the year, providing they do it in a constructive way, is always preferable to a boss who never says you are doing anything wrong or fails to identify areas you can build upon.

3. ASKING YOU QUESTIONS

'How are you feeling?', 'Is there anything I can be doing to help you?', 'Have I done anything to upset or frustrate you?', 'Are you worried or unsure about anything at all?' All of these are great questions for your manager to be asking, and it all boils down to the same green flag: does your boss actually ask you questions and do they listen to what you tell them?

Bosses that give you the feeling that they are genuinely listening to you when you speak is a great sign. Not least because it often leads to productive conversations around how to move both you and the business forward.

One of the very first points I made in this chapter was how many workplace issues are caused by misunderstandings and poor communication as much as from genuine intent. A boss that takes the time to ask the right questions and listen to the responses is always going to be more likely to mitigate this risk. They will have the unvarnished truth of how someone is feeling and be able to respond accordingly. They might not always take the decision that you want, but good business owners know that a hacked-off team rarely leads to an uptick in revenue or profit so will respond accordingly.

4. TAKING THE EMOTION OUT OF IT

I watch a huge amount of sport: football, cricket, rugby, golf. I can pretty much throw myself in front of anything and enjoy it. Despite it being one of my favourite things to do, I have found myself increasingly driven up the wall by the commentary from supposed experts that accompanies it.

Commentators and half-time analysis are supposed to be providing us with meaningful insights that we, the non-experts, would be unable to arrive at on our own.

And yet too often, instead of an actual discussion of tactics, we are forced to listen to unhelpful comments such as 'they just wanted it more' and 'a win is a win' and other gems that make some of the posts you see on LinkedIn look informative.

The one comment they usually throw out recklessly, that I agree with wholeheartedly, is commending teams and players with experience. Not necessarily because experience will always win, but because it gives you perspective to allow you to keep your cool and not lose your shit in the moment leading to a costly moment for your team.

Good management and bosses are like that. The best bosses take the emotion out of feedback sessions and offer perspective.

I am not saying they should be robots. Empathy and understanding are always going to be key to engaging effectively with employees, but you want to feel like your boss is not someone who is going to get upset, worried or in general too affected by anything you say. They should be able to handle anything you bring up and deal with it in a professional manner that allows you to move forwards, ideally with whatever issue you have raised being resolved.

5. FOLLOWING UP

This is wildly underutilised as an option by managers. Much like if a tree falls down and no one hears it, if feedback is agreed and nothing is recorded then it is much more likely never to materialise.

And this isn't me suggesting your boss will deliberately ignore any promises they made or anything as malevolent as that. There are of course those complete liars who will promise you something with no intention of ever delivering, but far more common is just the fact that a year is a long time and things get forgotten.

This is especially true when you think about the fact that if you are having proper one-to-ones you are essentially having 26 meetings with your manager over the course of a year. I don't care if they are the most insightful, entertaining and thought-provoking meetings of your life, 26 meetings is too many without any written record of what you actually discussed.

This is a great moment where you can start taking a bit more responsibility for your own career. As ever, it would of course be helpful if your boss loosely stepped up to do what they should be doing but, if they don't send a follow-up email, you taking that on is a really smart move; not least because a lot of the feedback I get from people who do this is that this is a really good way to solidify what you need to do in your mind and keep you focused on the areas that you need to improve.

Just a simple follow-up email highlighting the areas that you have been told you are doing well, areas you need to focus on, flagging any issues you are having and then a couple of lines saying whether you are on track to hit your targets overall. This will take you no more than five minutes to do, but will have an enormous impact when it comes to having those more important conversations about pay and promotions.

WORK–LIFE BALANCE

Boss: Heyyy Jen! I need you to cover a shift for me this Sunday. That cool?

Employee: Hey, so sorry but I can't. I've got plans and I've already done ten days straight. Sunday is my saviour right now lol.

Boss: I am really sorry, but I really need you to do this. We're short-staffed and you're the only one I trust to cover shifts when I'm not in. I will try and get you some time off next weekend.

Employee: You know I would if I could, but James and I haven't had time off together in a while and we have plans. I'm sure the others will be fine without us for a day :).

Boss: You're really putting me in a bind here. Need you to be a bit more of a team player.

As my wife is so quick to point out, I have always been a creature of habit. The sort of person who, once he has stumbled across a structure that works, will happily stick to it for the rest of his life. I'm not proud of it, and I do try to push against it on occasion, but considering there is an Ethiopian food stall near me which sees me visit every weekend without fail come rain or shine, it becomes harder and harder to make a valid case against this.

It is to my eternal relief that this habitual lifestyle isn't something that has ever seeped into my professional career. I have never been someone who has feared change in the workplace. Don't get me wrong, the list of flaws I do have as a business leader is so long that it would make this book look like a pamphlet, but the one small scrap of comfort is that I have never found myself saying phrases such as 'this is just the way we have always done it'.

In fact, if I'm being completely honest with myself, when I was running my first business, I had more the opposite problem where we would jump from new idea to new idea and I would find myself frequently saying things like 'holy shit, we definitely can't do it that way again, what else have we got?'

The reality is that we as humans don't tend to stand still. Whether it is art, music, language, new generations bring new trends, new tastes and, while the older generations might grumble about how the old ways were better, there is a general acceptance that to stand still is to go backwards.

The workplace is no different. Things change; what was fresh and exciting becomes stale and tedious and companies either learn to accept change or fall by the wayside. And one of the biggest changes to working culture and working life has been the rise of the idea of work–life balance. In fact, I would go as far as to say it has had the biggest impact on work since the invention of the internet and email.

What is interesting is just how quickly this idea has been supercharged. The phrase wasn't even invented until the eighties as part of the Women's Liberation Movement and for decades afterwards it was looked at by most as a complete joke. The irony is that when the term was first used by this movement it was about trying to bring more into the 'work' part of work–life balance, with women feeling they weren't getting a fair shot at a proper career due to the expectations that women would have to prioritise being the primary manager of the household first, and career second.

These days it appears that the pendulum has swung in the other direction, with people feeling like they should have a right to an actual life outside of their careers. A survey from 2023 by Hays shows that 56 per cent of employees would take lower pay in return for a healthier work–life balance and 33 per cent consider it the most important factor. It has also become one of the biggest sources of friction between bosses and their teams. What is so silly about it is that, as ever with these types of problems, very few people disagree. Having a healthy balance in your personal life so that you can do your best work in your professional life is not exactly controversial. Yet it is at the centre of some of the most toxic and ridiculous stories that I have ever heard.

The role of Covid

The pandemic supercharged the prominence of the work–life balance discourse. While I think we were always heading that way, Covid rewrote working models so substantially that it caused a lot of workers to briefly come up for air and, in doing so, decide that they didn't fancy diving straight back down.

For all the jokes about the new snowflake generations, an

astonishing number of people in their fifties decided during the pandemic that they didn't fancy going back to work. The Office for National Statistics stated that three in five over-fifties left the workforce sooner than planned. And that wasn't anything to do with them suddenly becoming lazy. For the first time in decades, they had a moment of peace to recognise that what they actually wanted to do was less work and that they would settle for less money in return for more freedom.

Covid was the petrol thrown onto the work–life balance fire. It didn't change the direction of where we ended up, but it super-charged it, introducing a number of working life features that a lot of companies and bosses simply hadn't had any time to adjust to or comprehend. Flexible working, remote training and other phrases that sent shivers down their spines suddenly cropped up overnight and even the most nimble of businesses struggled to get a handle on it.

When work–life balance breaks down

Since the pandemic has receded and we have 'gone back to nor-mal', a lot of bosses have started to restrict or remove some of the freedoms that teams had. This has caused an explosion of bad feelings, anger and resentment that has led to my inbox being filled with messages from both sides trying to make their point.

I think this provides important context as to why there are so many intense disputes between bosses and employees and why they have been so visceral. There is no other topic that generates as much tension. Let's explain where the main work–life balance misunderstandings come from and why so many companies get it wrong.

HYPOCRISY

The first and most important point is the rank hypocrisy we see on display so regularly. Too many bosses spend a lot of time and effort (and LinkedIn posts) talking about how they value their team and the importance of promoting a healthy work–life balance but then treat any challenges in your personal life as nothing but an inconvenience for your professional one. One story shared with me was about a boss saying that he felt a female employee's priorities were not right because she was too distracted by her sick child in the hospital. Can you imagine being so deluded that you think someone is going to consider a salaried job to be more important than their ill child?

It is similar to people online who spend their life banging on about free speech and then lose their shit when someone says something that they disagree with. You can't have it both ways. Either a boss is in favour of promoting a work–life balance which means embracing the challenges that come with it or they are not.

The rise of business leaders having their own personal brand and social channels is not insignificant to this general feeling of frustration. Bosses being unsympathetic to your personal lives is not a new phenomenon. But bosses who are unsympathetic to your personal lives but then brag online about how amazing their team's social lives are is new, and it is really starting to rankle people.

If you've ever read negative Glassdoor reviews you will often see quoted the disconnect between what the boss says they are doing and what in fact happens. One of my personal favourites was the former employee who simply wrote: 'The best way to understand this business is to simply read what the CEO writes on his LinkedIn and assume the opposite. Worst place to work ever.'

LONGEVITY

This disconnect and resulting frustrations become even more apparent when longevity comes into it. A lot of managers love longevity. To a weird extent. I saw one idiot claim that he rejected any CV that had less than two years of service at any one company. Personally, I have never understood why people take how long you have worked at a company as such a core metric. What if in that year they accomplished more than anyone else could have done in three years? What if they are so good they can't be bothered to work for companies who aren't ambitious enough and have the confidence in their own abilities to leave a company that isn't good enough for them? One of the best marketing people I have ever met works for companies for 18 months and then quits. He loves coming into a company, restarting their entire marketing, getting it all up and running and, once it is done, he gets bored and leaves for pastures new. And yet under this complete moron's approach to CVs, he would look at this candidate's CV and say 'no thanks'. How can that possibly make sense?

The irony is that the correlation between the boss who judges

CVs this way and those who run businesses where people rarely stay beyond the two-year mark is suspiciously high.

But if longevity is so important, and if you are going to try and get people to stay for a considerable amount of time and commit a decent chunk of their career, then the reality is that employees should be rewarded for it and incentivised to stay. And at some point, something will happen in your employees' lives that will impact their work. It could be something exciting like a wedding or a child that means your job becomes a little less important in a priority sense, or it can be something tragic like an injury or an illness in the family. The best bosses recognise that if you give people actual support in those moments, they will repay you with hard work and loyalty for years, but if your boss is one of those people who somehow make an already impossible situation worse, they will find themselves losing team members hand over fist.

BURNOUT

Another challenge in this area is the idea of burnout. When work has reached such a tipping point that employees are so physically and/or emotionally exhausted they often have to step out of work altogether. It is something that has been on the rise these last few years and, inevitably, the root cause of why is an area of a lot of column inches and social media arguments about what the difference is between actual burnout and just being a bit run down. Some of the more belligerent entries into this debate reject it altogether, saying that it is just snowflakes being psychologically weak.

I find this particular view as unhelpful as it is idiotic. Some of the toughest people I know have very much suffered from burnout. No one is seriously going to look me in the eye and suggest that people like Ben Stokes and Simone Biles, who very famously admitted to burnout, are not mentally strong considering what they have accomplished in their sporting careers.

The problem is that we are all different. If we all had a burnout score of 100 and every different work–life factor impacted us all equally then we would be able to have a more rational discussion about it. But the reality is that we are all impacted in different ways and, as such, the barometer for measuring these types of things is subjective. With that debate comes the inevitable frustrations of feeling misunderstood and as if your boss or company don't care about your mental wellbeing.

THE GENERATIONAL FIGHT

The next part of the work–life balance argument is lobbed, as ever, at the younger generation's feet. The reality is that we in the West are suffering from productivity issues. The Office for National Statistics states that the UK's productivity is 26 per cent lower than it should be post-financial crisis. Now a lot of clever economists and experts will tell you that this is because of a chronic lack of investment in capital, but if you open up Twitter/X or check certain Facebook groups, you will be told it is because of how 'woke' the next generation of workers are, and how they are afraid of a hard day's work.

One of my favourite social media videos I've filmed was someone reading out how each generation thought the one that followed them was lazy, with newspaper clippings going back all the way to the eighteenth century. The idea that people think the juniors coming through are made of weaker stuff than they were is hardly a fresh take, but it simply isn't because they don't want to work hard. A survey funded by Apeiron Ventures found that Gen Z are among the most entrepreneurial generation we have ever had, with over 60 per cent thinking about starting their own business. What is accurate however, is that younger generations are a lot more aware of what is and isn't acceptable and what they are willing to sacrifice from a mental health perspective for their careers.

A lot of the workforce these days is choosing to take less stressful jobs and turning away promotions, not because they aren't ambitious or that they don't want to succeed, but in recognition that it is not the complete end goal and other parts of your life should, at the very least, be fairly represented. Alongside this fact, the rise of social media and the internet has made it so much easier to start your own business, giving you more options. This means that the younger generations can look at some of the more toxic traits that older generations had to put up with from bosses and managers and think, *Yeah no thanks, I will do my own thing.*

The problem we have is that we are in a pretty unmotivated time when it comes to approaching work, and because morale is so low it is easy just to say 'work is never going to be fun, we just have to suffer through it'. But I completely disagree with that. I think the best jobs and companies provide a workplace which can genuinely give you a purpose, making you feel like you are contributing to something and feeling so much better about yourself because of it.

That being said, your career is a marathon not a sprint and, while there will always be times where your professional life is impacting your personal life, it is not sustainable to have that inequality for too long because, not only will your personal life suffer, but it will eventually catch up to your professional life as well.

The best companies are fully aware of this. They understand fundamentally that it is in their own commercial interests to make sure their team has that right balance as much as it is the right thing to do.

However, sadly there are many who act in bad faith. The challenge is that they can be quite hard to spot. While it would be easier to spot a bad boss if they went around saying, 'I don't give a flying fuck about my team's personal life', sadly they are just clever enough to recognise that wouldn't go down too well for them, and so they will all mostly say the right things, meaning it is in their actions that we have to catch them out.

And so what can you do to identify those companies who have little to no respect for your personal life? What are the warning signs that you are starting to feel the pressure and what can you do to get that balance back so you can fulfil your potential at work?

Red flags to watch out for

1. TOO MUCH WORK – NOT ENOUGH LIFE

WhatsApp has featured more prominently than I expected in this book when I started writing it. And it feels unlikely that what

I have written about it is going to get me any postcards from Meta anytime soon because it hasn't come out of this smelling of roses. WhatsApp, whether intentionally or not, has bridged the gap between work comms and personal comms in a depressingly efficient way. While that gives you an easy way to chat to your boss, which has its strengths, it also makes it far too simple for them to send you 'just a quick one' at unhelpful hours of the day.

I am not saying that any boss who messages you out of hours is Satan in corporate form, but any leader or manager who consistently does this will find a red flag attached to their name pretty sharpish, even if 'it is just a small favour' which, as an FYI, it very rarely is.

There are two reasons why I dislike this so much. It shows a real lack of respect for you as an employee, which is never a great sign for your career prospects; and if a business is constantly requiring you to do things in the evenings and the weekends it suggests a chaos to the company which should worry you from a stability perspective.

The sad thing about this one in particular is that it sneaks up on you, and before you know it, you're not only answering work messages at home, you're stuck in the office after-hours. In fact, a friend of mine was recently celebrating because 'he only had to work late twice this week' as though he had been given a real treat.

As ever, for me it comes down to choice. If you want to prioritise your career above all else and absolutely throw yourself into it, working weekends and evenings, then that is your choice and you will hear nothing but admiration and support from me about it. But it has to be your choice to want to do it. Any boss who is forcing you is just going to end up ruining your motivation, which will have a ripple effect across the business.

2. COMPLETE DISREGARD OF ANNUAL LEAVE

If there is one lesson you take away from this chapter, it is that just because a boss asks you to do something nicely, doesn't mean it is OK.

Messing around with annual leave usually comes in two main forms.

a. You are bombarded with requests despite supposedly being on, what's the word, oh yes, holiday.

b. Bosses make it difficult to book the holiday off in the first place. Whether it is trying to swap holidays which you had already booked off months ago, or acting like a complete diva in the build up to you going away, making it feel like you have run over their cat, rather than simply booking a little time off as you are very much allowed to do.

What I find interesting is that the modern day boss is fully aware they shouldn't be doing this. Whereas before we had the clichéd boss our parents told us about who screamed and shouted and threw staplers at people's heads, we are now into the second generation of annual leave disrupters, where they rely on guilt and the kindness of your heart to get what they want.

The one exception that I have found is American law firms. Honestly, they are just terrible to the point at which it is almost comedic. Easily one of the worst sectors that you can work in.

And yes, I know the pay is phenomenal, but you get about four hours a month to yourself with which to spend it.

3. ASSIGNING TASKS LATE AND EXPECTING THEM TO BE DONE THAT DAY

The defence that I hear, and I do use that word loosely, is that bosses often don't realise how much time some things take. They have so little idea about your work capacity and the work itself that they don't realise how big a task they have assigned you. If I have a manager or a team leader at my company handing out tasks with little to no idea of what they involve, they will not find themselves in charge for very long.

One of your core roles as a manager is to ensure your team's time is being spent efficiently, so how on earth are you meant to be doing that if you are handing out jobs with no idea of the time required?

So it doesn't matter if the bosses don't care or if they simply don't know, this is an enormous red flag and a clear sign they have zero respect for any sort of personal life balance.

4. HOW THEY ACT WHEN SOMETHING HAPPENS IN YOUR LIFE

This is a big one. One story recently shared with me recounted an employee whose husband was literally dying in hospital after being in an accident and her boss, fully aware of the situation, had called her four times to check to see if she would be at work on Monday.

Just pause for a moment, and reread that sentence.

Can you imagine the mind of someone who, a) thinks that this is even a remotely acceptable thing to do and, b) thinks anyone could give two hoots about work when they are going through something like this? And that is the point. It is an extreme story, but it makes my argument perfectly.

5. PRAISING OVERWORK AS DEDICATION

I understand the instinct of a boss who praises the number of hours being worked. If someone really has put in a real shift, it is a perfectly natural thing to do and not something to be criticised in isolation.

The challenge I have with it is the logic behind it. If, for example, two people do the same task, but one does it in four hours and the other in eight, should the person who took eight be praised over the person who did it quicker? Of course not.

Bosses who think that the people who stay the latest in the office are their best employees are just completely misunderstanding how to track what makes a good employee. One of the best sales people I have ever worked with was, and he is a friend of mine so I get to say this, the laziest git you will ever meet. He would loaf about the office for half the day, would be distracted by the tiniest interruption and in every sense of the word was hopeless beyond a very small two- or three-hour window in which he would concentrate.

It just so happened that, during those two or three hours he weaved absolute magic, delivering more revenue to the company than anyone else and consistently coming top in the sales he would achieve.

Now I am not saying we should be hanging his picture under the 'perfect employee' sign anytime soon, but the principle here is that the best bosses value their employees on the actual output and the quality that they deliver, rather than just who stayed the latest in the office. Praise what has been done, but never celebrate how long it has taken.

The other obvious point is this is especially a red flag if this same boss spends his or her life bleating about how important work–life balance is and how they always make sure to prioritise that. People always forget to think about what that means.

6. IT'S CALLED 'ON CALL' FOR A REASON

This one annoys me no end. The expectation for teams to always be available even when they are not actually contracted to be is as short-sighted as it is unfair. Essentially looking for all the requirements of being on call with none of the financial rewards.

Unlike a lot of the nonsense phrases that get bandied around the office that sound impressive but are completely meaningless – 'lateral thinking', 'touching base' and many more – 'on call' has a legitimate definition. It means you are paying someone to be available should a requirement come up. Yet the paying part of this seems to be conveniently forgotten as bosses essentially line up people to always be available to work.

Instead, the compensation you receive tends to be of the more biblical kind, mostly avoiding guilt and the wrath of your seniors.

It frustrates me further that so many companies think that they need this. There was an entrepreneur who was complaining, saying 'what if I have an emergency at 4.00am that I need someone to look at?' To which the obvious answer is, if you have that many emergencies at that time then you are operating in the wrong time zone.

Top signs that your personal life is out of whack with your professional one

1. TIREDNESS

There are times when you are fully aware of why you are tired. A late night with friends, one too many after work. And then there are the times you wake up feeling incredibly hard done by. You have gone to bed early, slept like the dead and still feel completely shattered.

This can be one of the biggest signs that you are approaching the end of your limits. This, combined with a lack of motivation, is one of the surefire signs that your work has got to a point where it is negatively impacting your health and wellbeing and it really is important you recognise that and don't try and simply 'power through'.

2. CYNICISM TOWARDS WORK

'What is the point of my job?' This is, at the best of times, a dangerous thread to pull on. We live in a world where the vast majority of people's jobs seem relatively pointless when you really look at what they do, especially the more city-based ones. And I very much include myself in this. In fact, I am even worse, my job is to talk about these pointless jobs, which makes my role useless once removed.

My existential crisis to one side though, how you feel about your work is a great way to take a quick snapshot of where your head is currently at and how you are feeling in general.

3. INCREASED USE OF COPING MECHANISMS

We all have our vices. Some of us drink, some of us smoke, some of us post cryptocurrency conspiracies on Reddit. Some of us, irritatingly, have somehow managed to establish healthy vices like running or cycling.

Either way, one of the best signs that you are out of whack at work is a feeling like you are becoming over-reliant on those vices. If you find yourself craving them rather than simply wanting to do them, that is usually a sign you are growing more dependent due to work not even remotely giving you what you need.

4. LOWER TOLERANCE FOR IRRITATION OR ANGER

I once worked with someone who would simply drive me up the wall. To this day I have no idea why. They were, on paper, a lovely human being. But there was just something about them that rubbed me up the wrong way. I mean to the extent where I could have a three-month sabbatical, where all I did was sway gently in a hammock on a tropical island listening to whale noises, and they would still have me tearing my hair out within minutes of being back in their company.

Not everyone is like that though. If you feel like you are being shorter with your colleagues, or find yourself feeling more irritated with your day-to-day dealings, then my honest advice would be to book a holiday as soon as you can. Not least because, even if you don't do it for you, do it for your colleagues, because having someone like that working with you on a day-to-day basis can have a ripple effect that drags everyone down.

What should you do to get the balance back?

1. IDENTIFY WHERE YOU ARE STRUGGLING

This sounds like it should be relatively straightforward but it isn't always the case, and it is such a critical part of getting yourself back on track. It could be something obvious like the number of hours you are working, or someone at work who is making your life particularly hellish.

It could equally be something a bit more obscure. Boredom is the one that people struggle to identify the most. Feeling challenged is such an important part of enjoying a job, and so I would try and volunteer to get involved in a part of the business that you haven't done before or ask to take on something more challenging to counter this if you are feeling bored.

2. SPEAK TO YOUR BOSS

Now I am fully aware that if you are feeling like your personal life is being impacted by your professional life, there is a strong chance that your boss is going to feature heavily in the story as to why that is. And if they are one of those who truly do just lose their temper at the slightest provocation then I would tell you to leave.

But if your boss is the cause, statistically speaking, they will more likely be causing you issues through ignorance (like we have mentioned throughout this book) so it is worth having those moments of complete honesty.

Don't be accusatory because the second someone feels like they are being blamed, they will go on the defensive. If you are thinking of leaving anyway, there is absolutely nothing to lose in being completely honest about what is bothering you and seeing if there is something that can be done.

The best approach to this meeting is really to think about what you are looking for from an outcome perspective. If you go in with broad statements such as 'I want to feel less drained' then it is going to be really difficult to arrive at a solution that works. Whereas if you said, for example, 'I was wondering if I could start work half an hour earlier so that I can extend my lunch break and give myself a chance to go to the gym, which I think will put me in a better headspace.' That is something a lot more focused that you can have an honest chat about practically.

3. BE PROACTIVE

This is the time to start really taking the lead and prioritising yourself. Whether it is booking a holiday, ensuring that you start leaving work on time, picking up a new hobby, finding solace in the arms of an old hobby; whatever it is that you do to start making yourself feel more like you, should be your one and only goal. If you don't feel like any of your current habits are helping then try some new ones. Padel is sweeping the world right now and I would personally highly recommend it. Equally, if you are unfit, but want to kid yourself and pretend that you are exercising, Pickleball is a great alternative.

As a small note, I think it says everything you need to know about Pickleball players that, in a book where I have called out several of the largest and most powerful companies in the world, this is the joke I am most worried about.

4. LEAVE

It isn't worth it. Honestly, I really do mean that. There is no job in the world that is worth feeling shit for. You can read all of the LinkedIn posts about how it is worth sacrificing everything for your career and to follow the plan no matter the cost etc., but 1) LinkedIn rivals Twitter/X during an election when it comes to reliability; 2) most of the people who post these sorts of things have never taken their own advice; and, 3) it is so unlikely you will achieve any sort of meaningful success if you have no life and are completely miserable.

I am not saying you jump straight to this. It is always worth trying to get things back on track, especially if you used to love where you work because that is worth at least attempting to rediscover. However, ultimately, if it doesn't work, sometimes the best cure is just a new role with a new company. We are all creatures of habit sometimes but, when it comes down to it, it is the new that we find most exciting, and when it comes to making it feel like your work has balance, excitement is one of the best things to pursue.

QUITTING

Boss: *I need you to come in tomorrow I am afraid.*

Employee: *But it's my day off?*

Boss: *I know, and I am sorry about that, but there's nothing I can do. We are light on people.*

Employee: *You can't make me come in at such short notice.*

Boss: *You know that I can, don't be unhelpful, this situation is stressful enough as it is.*

Employee: *Sounds like a you problem. I quit.*

I have never been a big runner. I love sport, and I've played everything from rugby, cricket and football, to hockey. It has dominated a huge part of both my childhood and adult life.

But running I have always found to be incredibly tedious. Trotting along from point A to B without being able to throw, catch or kick something is excruciatingly boring. It has always meant that I have found other ways to say fit (ish).

The advent of a dodgy knee in my late twenties gave me an actual excuse to latch onto; 'I wish I could run more, but my knee just can't take it these days' I can now say, as though I was out there pounding the pavement when I had two fully functioning knees.

On the rare occasion I do drag myself out there, I turn to an old playlist that I always fire up. The first song is The Clash's 'Should I Stay or Should I Go'. And, much like the self-reflection I face every time I pull my trainers on, when it comes to your job, it is often not as clear as you might think.

I have never loved the word 'quit' when it comes to work. There is just too much of a 'giving up' connotation, which I think is a distinctly unhelpful contribution to what is, already, an incredibly stressful and anxiety-filled time. In a book of ridiculous stories and terrible puns you might not expect a huge amount of serious-ness, but on this particular point, I am deadly serious when I say that leaving a job can be one of the bravest things you can ever do.

This is especially true when the root cause of why you are quit-ting is a boss or colleague. The feeling of dread in the pit of your stomach, that awful sensation of not wanting to get out of bed because of a genuine fear to face the day; to summon the courage to get yourself out of that requires a huge strength of character. To use the same word 'quit' with the ease with which my brother decided to stop playing the clarinet feels like a let-down.

For anyone who is in that position, I can't tell you how import-ant it is to get out of there and I hope this book and my work provide you some comfort and support.

But what if you kind of like your job but feel as if you are going nowhere? Or enjoy the work but can't stand your boss? What if you believe you are kidding yourself to think there is better any-where else? That is what this chapter is looking to answer: the question Joe Strummer would shout at me over and over as I grumpily slogged around my running route; I didn't stay, I went.

Things to think about before you do quit

While emphasising how many legitimate reasons there are for leaving your job, and why it is so often the right move, I am now going to inject a small piece of caution by covering what you need to think about before you actually pull the trigger and hand in your notice.

The first is obvious: what is the risk to you financially? If you leave your job for another, and it doesn't work out, or if you leave and you don't have another opportunity lined up, how long financially will you be able to keep going? If you earn no income for three months for example, do you have the savings to look after yourself? It could be that it is worth sticking out for a little bit longer until you either have enough saved up, or you have a clear opportunity all agreed so that you can have the confidence to move on.

'Quiet quitting' has been making the news, and not always in a good way, but I genuinely see no issue with it. Having employed people for the last ten years, I have always taken the view that it is on the boss to motivate people to work in the way that they want. If they have failed to do that, then that is their problem, not the poor soul languishing beneath them.

The premise of this is incredibly simple. It is when an employee does everything to the letter of the contract but no more. They will show up on time, they will deliver the core responsibilities but will simply not do any more beyond that. No working late, no additional duties. They will do the absolute bare minimum to ensure they are not fired but will not lift a finger to do anything else.

This has caused a real culture clash between a lot of bosses and employees as you can imagine. From my side, as so often with these types of things, I always prefer to flip this back on the boss or the manager and ask these very simple questions: why does no one want to go above and beyond for you? Are you incentivising them enough? Are you causing issues in how they do their work which is demotivating them? Or maybe they have something going on in their life that is impacting their work?

Either way I don't have a huge amount of sympathy for bosses who complain about this because I view it as their role to provide the motivation to deliver the best work, not simply to expect people to show up to work for them already fired up. It is their job to know what is going on.

For example, I had a boss complaining about how he felt his team wasn't producing as much as it used to and then it turned out that someone had handed in their notice and left the company without him realising. I don't even know what you would call that – 'quietest quitting' maybe?

Anyway, this memorable meeting finished with him having the gall to say that he would have noticed this person had left if everyone didn't want to work from home these days. Another win for the 'taking responsibility' brigade.

The second piece of advice I would give you if you are thinking about quitting your job is to spend time doing some proper market research and thinking about what it is you want. What are you actually looking for and is it even possible to achieve it? Write out a clear list of objectives of what you would like to be doing in five years' time and then do some proper due diligence of what it is you need to achieve in order to get it. This is especially relevant if you are looking to move careers along with finding a new job.

And just in case you aren't aware of this, by research I am not talking about a quick google on your phone while you binge the latest season of *Below Deck*. I am talking about genuine in-depth study, using everything from YouTube, articles, surveys and, if you are feeling particularly brave, conversations with other people both already in your network or reaching out to people on platforms such as LinkedIn. The reason why this is so important is that, firstly, it gives you the information to understand what your value on the market is and the best way to highlight that and, secondly, it might give you a clue as to how valued you are at your current role.

Thirdly, do a proper skills assessment of what it is you can do, especially if you have been at one company for a while. A lot of companies have helpfully decided to break completely from societal norms and, in some more extreme cases, actual sanity, when it comes to job titles and job descriptions. What you do day-to-day may not be what you will be required to do in a new job at a fresh company, even if the title sounds the same.

This can work in your favour, where people have been underpaid compared to the level of seniority they perform at. I had one memorable conversation with someone who applied to a company as a junior network engineer and came out of the interview slightly baffled because he had been offered the head of department role. I would call this a win, but considering he had been underpaid for the last three years that feels a bit rich. Equally though, it could be that, for whatever reason, you are lacking in a couple of key areas and if you move and discover you aren't able to fulfil the job requirements, you could end up unemployed.

Finally, get some external advice from other people in the industry to find out exactly how bad your current boss or company is. You might think the place you work in is nothing short of diabolical, however if this is the only company you have ever worked in, or if you are still relatively new to the industry, you do not have enough comparison points to make that objective call.

Again, meet people in person. Reach out to friends or ask for introductions to people in your network, offer to take them for a coffee, or a drink, and say 'this is where I am struggling, this is why I want to leave' and listen and see if they agree with you.

When you shouldn't quit

I am a big believer in people leaving their jobs. The definition of madness, as widely attributed to Einstein, is to do the same thing over and over and expect a different result, and if a company consistently lets you down, then it is unlikely that they are suddenly going to turn a corner.

That being said, there are a few scenarios where you absolutely should not quit or, at the very least, give it a little bit of time before you make that decision.

Firstly, if you have no idea what you are going to do next, then take a pause. The exception to this rule is when you are feeling so lost and beaten down that you can't see the wood for the trees and need a couple of months off just to get there. Otherwise, my advice would be to pull back at work where you can, and start to think about what you would want to do if you were to hand in your notice.

The second reason why you shouldn't quit is because you are annoyed or feeling some other heightened emotion. Especially anger. A lot of people say anger is a good thing. That it drives you to succeed, fuelling the hunger for everything that you want to accomplish. That might be true, but I am not so convinced.

Regardless, it absolutely has no place in being the reason you are quitting. I am not saying not to quit at all, I am saying take a day or two for the heat to burn down a little bit and then assess if quitting is still the right thing to do. Trust me, if it is a good enough reason, it will still look valid in a colder light.

You want to talk to your boss before you leave, too. Once you've quit, you've quit. It is such a final decision that it is always worth throwing a bit of a Hail Mary and speaking to your employer before you make that final call.

The reason why I like this is, a) there is no downside because if they are unable to help with your queries or issues, you will be quitting anyway, and in fact you will have a clearer conscience about it; and, b) you are in a position of power if you have a new gig lined up. It means you can ask for what you want rather than what you think they might say yes to.

Whether it is money, moving to a new team, a bit more

flexibility, there is absolutely no harm in asking. The worst they can do is say no, but there is always a possibility they can move things around to accommodate your demands.

The final reason is if something big is going on outside of work. Life will sometimes just kick you in the teeth. I know this is meant to be a motivating book that gives you advice and that warm feeling that you are not alone in going through work hell, but one of the sad facts of having a career that will span several decades is that, at some point, things will happen in your personal life that will leak into your professional one.

The most common reaction is to lose interest in work completely. This is understandable. If someone significant in your life is ill or has passed away, Deborah's monthly email reminders to track time and to submit your monthly reports pale to a level of total insignificance.

The reality is, when something like that is happening, this is not the time to be making big life decisions. Of course, if circumstance dictates you need to quit for family reasons that is totally different, but if it is more of a morale-dictated decision then it is worth holding off.

You will notice with all these reasons that the common theme is giving yourself time. It is about protecting you and your job as much as anything else, and, while companies will often talk a good game about supporting you through something like this, the reality is that once you hand in your notice, it is extremely rare you will get an opportunity to take that back. And so, you want to make sure it is absolutely the right decision for you.

Reasons why you absolutely should quit

1. BOREDOM

There is nothing quite as dispiriting as being bored at work. Now don't get me wrong, every job has boring moments, monthly reports, admin style paperwork etc. Those little tedious moments that keep the cogs of any business going.

I am not even talking about tasks that you might find tedious but others enjoy. A good example of this is one of my best friends who works as an accountant and he spent a memorable six months of one year heading up to Swindon once a week to audit gravel.

I mean, technically it wasn't just gravel, it was sand, rock and a bunch of other materials but if you are arguing about which type of sediment you are meant to be auditing then, in my humble opinion, you have already lost the argument. But he seemed to enjoy it. Though he also quit a year later so 'enjoy' might be quite a strong word here.

No, I am talking about the 'been there and done that' feeling, that sense that your day-to-day role is so ingrained, you could do the majority of it on autopilot.

A simple test I recommend is to consider the last 12–18 months in the job and think of the moments you were excited or nervous about. If you cannot point to an example, it's time to think about new opportunities.

Careers are a marathon not a sprint. There will be times you want to go all guns blazing and, perhaps after a tough few years or maybe if you have a lot going on in your personal life, you might be happy to take a low-effort role. But if that is the case you won't be feeling bored.

Being tested at work is important. If you are not, then not only will you start to feel unmotivated to do even the basics, that apathy can also easily contaminate your colleagues and end up dragging down the whole team. If you are in this position, the easiest way to shake it up is to change your surroundings via a new challenge or job.

2. TOXIC WORKPLACE

We once had a bullying talk at our school. Not that I went to a particularly tough school. Technically, we did have a school bully. But he used to go bird watching at the weekends so it wasn't exactly Rikers Island.

I remember one of the phrases that they used when explaining how to handle being bullied: 'No one heals himself by wounding another'. While that might technically be true, judging by some of the stories that have been shared with me recently, I would say that there are a depressing amount of people out there who are giving it a bloody good go.

The combination of really liking your job but it being utterly ruined by someone at work is a particularly bitter source of pain. This is because if you hate your job, and your colleagues, and your boss and everything about the company, then choosing to leave becomes incredibly easy. When there is just one source of pain standing between you and what could be a really great gig, then there is a tendency to try and stick it out for that bit longer, hoping things will get better.

The honest truth is that unless that person leaves, the chances of it getting better are almost zero. 'People can change' looks great on a mug, but when it comes to people who make the lives of others miserable, especially if they are more senior, it just doesn't happen. Leaving your job is absolutely the right decision and you can do so with absolutely no regrets.

3. JOB MISALIGNMENT

Certain bosses and managers seem to be under the fairly strange perception that they can hire someone to do a specific job and then just change it once they have been hired.

They seem to be genuinely surprised when people get a little bit hacked off by this particular piece of skulduggery.

Someone who messaged me was promised a head of department role, signed a contract saying as much, and joined to find out that the company had already hired a head of department and that they wanted her to take the deputy role instead. She handed in her notice before the first week was up. What a pointless waste of time that is for everyone involved, but especially her who then had to start her job search all over again, this time without her existing employment.

If a business tries to change your job through either scope creep or suddenly, you should not feel obliged to stick it out if you don't want to. Dust off your CV and start applying before the ink on your new spec has even dried.

4. WORK–LIFE BALANCE

There is no magic ratio for work–life balance because we are all different and, more importantly, our priorities shift at various points in our career. For example, when you are first starting out you might want to make a big early push as opposed to when you have a young family and want to see more of them.

Therefore, me saying something like 'you want to have two social events with friends for every three hours of extra work you do for your boss' would be completely pointless. 'You want to stroke a black cat for every ten emails you receive' would be just as helpful a ratio to go for, if not a little bit more because at least that way you might have banked a bit of feline good luck.

Whether your current work–life balance is worthy of quitting your job over or not is based on two questions. Am I feeling happy about my current workload at the moment? And, if not, how much longer can I go at this pace? Sometimes work just gets busy. Whatever the reason, we can all progress through the gears when we need to. The key is working out how long you think you can maintain that pace. It is the equivalent of going from a slow jog to an all-out sprint; it is doable, but recognise at what point you will reach the end of your endurance.

If you are tapped out before your workload starts to reduce, then you need to leave, it is as simple as that. Listen to your body and how you are feeling. Burnout symptoms don't always materialise in the most obvious of ways. I am a great example of this. During Covid when my business's clients were cancelling work left, right and centre, I started to get what I thought were Covid-like symptoms, disregarding the possibility that it was stress. It was only after a string of negative tests over five weeks in a row that my wife finally told me to stop being an idiot and to start looking after myself.

The final point I would say is that a lack of work–life balance can cause you some grief even with a boss you love. So, before you quit and if you do really like where you are working, speak to your employer, be completely upfront about where you are at, as they may be able to support you before you take that step.

5. UNDERVALUED AND UNAPPRECIATED

Nothing frustrates me more than a manager not giving praise where it is deserved or, even worse, stealing credit. It is just a terrible thing to do; the social equivalent of showing up an hour early to someone's house party. But the other reason why I get so frustrated is that it is just so short-sighted.

As a manager, your job, and therefore your success, is tied to how your team is doing. The better they perform, the more you are praised and the more significant your potential career advancement.

Now in an ideal world we would do a job simply for the plea-sure of doing a good job. The reality is that people need praise. We thrive on it. Feeling like you are doing a good job is almost always directly tied to external sources of validation, no matter how much we tell ourselves that we are fab and it doesn't matter what every-one else thinks.

A manager that steals your thunder just isn't someone you want to work with. If they are doing this, then they will be cocking up in other areas as well. This is a situation you want to duck out of as soon as possible.

6. ETHICAL CONCERNS

Sadly, companies are not always on their best behaviour.

It would be churlish of me to start naming companies or industries who I personally think are unethical. And so, with that in mind, I will not be mentioning vaping companies who absolutely do not advertise to under-eighteens in any way with their flavour range that specifically appeals to that age bracket. That is a massive coincidence. Vaping is just a way to help people stop smoking, a health service, which is of course why there are so many large players in that particular sector. But I digress. A company doing something that goes against what you really believe in is a hugely legitimate reason to leave a job. The realists among you will say that this is a luxury. That no business is perfect, and that unless you end up working for David Attenborough, then there will be nowhere for you to go. But I am not talking about things you find irritating. I am talking about your absolute core beliefs. Those three or four things that mean the world to you and are lines that you don't cross. If it is something that makes up a huge part of who you are, then forcing yourself to work for someone who stands for the complete opposite can impact you negatively.

It could be supporting social causes such as Pride or women's rights. It could be environmental, it could be based on religion, it could even be something incredibly niche and personal to you. I know of someone in the US who lost his home during the 2008 crash and has told me that he therefore refuses point blank to work for any bank that was involved.

You don't have to get on a soapbox about it; in fact, it is not fair at all to try and make people who remain at the company feel bad about themselves but I absolutely support anyone who makes the decision to leave based on their personal beliefs. In fact, I applaud people who do this.

7. BETTER OPPORTUNITIES ELSEWHERE

I cannot emphasise this point enough. The 'good bosses', or the ones who know how to run a competent team, will understand if you get a significantly better offer, whether that be monetary or with more progression that they cannot match and will not hold it against you. In fact, they will likely be pleased for you. I really do mean this.

If an opportunity arises elsewhere then there is no downside to taking it. The good bosses will be pleased for you and any boss that reacts poorly and takes it badly is not worth worrying about in the first place.

Ultimately your career has to be viewed selfishly.

You can be grateful to a company, you can miss them when you leave, you can love the people you work with, you can be proud of the output you delivered; in fact, it is great if you do all these things. But none of it means you should stay when you get a better opportunity. You in fact run the risk of building resentment that would tarnish your experience of working there anyway. If taking a new job is the best move for you, then it is nearly always the best move for both companies involved as well.

How to quit

I know the temptation for a lot of people is to stride into the room like Eduardo Saverin in *The Social Network*, sweep everything off their desk, tell them exactly where they can go and then, with two fingers raised, walk triumphantly off into the sunset.

My advice is not to give into that temptation. For one, the short-term gratification of telling your boss to go to hell will not outweigh the long-term damage that completely torpedoing that relationship might cause. And secondly, and something Hollywood films always seem to neglect to point out, you have something called a notice period which you will have to serve unless the company lets you leave earlier. So giving your boss both barrels before walking sheepishly back to your desk to settle down for another four weeks of work can become a little bit awkward.

Let's look at the step-by-step best way to quit, not forgetting what you need to look out for and how to do it in a way that will maximise your chance of getting the best out of what could well be a very tough situation.

STEP 1: BE ORGANISED

Make sure you have a handle on your details. The obvious point is to check your contract to make sure you know exactly what your notice period is and how long you will have to continue to work before you can leave.

Alongside this, make sure you check how much holiday you have taken, so you are aware if you have taken more than your annual allowance up until that point. For example, if you are halfway through the year when you quit but you have taken the equivalent of three-quarters of your annual leave allowance then you will be charged for those three months. People often message me having been surprised by this and say how unfair they believe it is, but it's actually very reasonable when you think about it.

Otherwise, those 'winter sun' deals you see being flogged by every airline under the sun would do a roaring trade as everyone would book three weeks off in January, max out their holiday, and then hand in their notice with very tanned arms at the end of the month.

The details are yours to own, and no one else's.

I had one person message me saying that his old company had cost him his new job because he didn't realise he had a month's notice period and the new company wanted him to start immediately. And while I have a huge amount of sympathy for him, it was absolutely his fault; the company was well within their rights to make him work his notice as they will often need that time to find a replacement. Plus, don't forget, the notice period is what prevents you being fired immediately and gives you that window to find a new job if the shoe is on the other foot.

On the flip side, if you haven't taken much holiday at all, they will technically owe you money and so you can use that as an opportunity to negotiate a shorter notice period.

STEP 2: DO IT FACE TO FACE

I appreciate we are in a new world of remote working, and so when I say face to face, it doesn't have to be in person, a video call is perfectly reasonable, however what I am getting at is this is a conversation that needs to happen first. Don't just drop an email in their inbox or, even worse, send them a text or message.

This isn't a legal requirement, it is just the right thing to do. Now I know that there are a lot of bosses out there people will feel aren't worthy of giving this respect to, and you could well be right, but just because someone else is an arsehole doesn't mean that you should stop trying to do the right thing. Otherwise the world starts to get pretty dark pretty quickly.

The other benefit is that it makes them address it straightaway, they can't claim they didn't see your email, or misinterpret what you are trying to say. Take the initiative, put some time in their diary or arrange a meeting.

STEP 3: FOCUS ON THE POSITIVES AS TO WHY YOU ARE LEAVING

The vast majority of the people who leave a job are doing it for negative reasons. An unreasonable workload, a toxic work culture, a boss who has decided that his team needs to take it in turns to buy a round of coffees each morning at $50 a pop with him being the only exception (I wish I was making this up).

However, the resignation meeting is not the time to bring all of this up. A good company will set up a proper exit interview at a later date for you to give them your feedback, and the bad companies will ignore your advice anyway, so it isn't worth the oxygen. Going back to the point about getting the best outcome for you, this is the time to focus on what you are moving to rather than what you are moving from.

'I am really excited about this new opportunity', 'I really want to go travelling'; whatever it might be (and feel free to make something up if you truly don't have something to go to yet) you don't want to give them an opportunity to start an argument or discuss whether you should move at all. It is imperative that you remember this is not a debate as to whether you should quit, it is you informing them that you are, and if you start talking about things like 'I don't like the way I am managed' or 'I haven't been enjoying work' you open the door to them starting to promise to fix those issues, or argue with you.

STEP 4: FOLLOW UP IMMEDIATELY IN WRITING

As soon as you leave the meeting, get everything in writing. Again, this is not the time to go into detail as to the whys of it all, and you do not even need to say where you are going. The important thing is to confirm the date you are serving your notice and the date you are leaving.

Do not give them any say on this. The trick is to confirm what your final day is in the email or letter you send to them. Put the onus on them to come back and disagree, do not let them start dictating when you leave as that again opens the door to them cajoling you.

One of the worst things that I have heard recently is a company that guilted this poor woman into staying an extra two months past her notice. They kept layering it on thick about how much she had let them down and that she owed them for leaving them in this spot. The fact that the reason she had left was because they had failed to give her a pay rise three years in a row didn't cross their minds as a contributing factor to her decision.

Do not let them do this. You have to work the notice, but you do not owe them anything beyond that, and any company that acts like you have done them a huge personal insult is not worth feeling guilty over.

STEP 5: HOLD AN EXIT INTERVIEW

Every company should have this as part of the process, however I am a big believer in offering to do this even if they haven't offered.

This is your chance to get a few things off your chest but, more importantly, you may have some genuine suggestions that could help both your colleagues who are still there, and the directors of the business make more informed decisions. I know social media often suggests the very contrary but people aren't deliberately terrible bosses and exit interviews are a really good way to give some honest feedback.

Again, don't get personal, focus on themes and keep it quite broad even if it is really obvious who you are talking about. This is about trying to make the business that little bit better rather than a courtroom to air every single thing that has hacked you off. Save that for the pub with your friends.

STEP 6: BE PROFESSIONAL IN YOUR NOTICE PERIOD

You can of course be excited about moving on, it would be weird if you weren't. But if you spend your notice acting like you have an Oasis ticket pre-dynamic pricing and that everyone who doesn't is missing out on the opportunity of their lifetime, then you are going to start coming across as a bit of an arsehole.

Remember, the goal of this is to get the best outcome for you. And the best outcome for you is the company respecting your efforts in the final weeks and your co-workers viewing you with affection. That means working hard and ensuring you make the first few days/weeks of your absence as easy as possible for everyone.

Offer to onboard the person replacing you, write out detailed handover docs and go above and beyond when it comes to walking people through the duties they might be taking over. This is such an important piece of advice because you can ruin years of good service if people feel like you are checking out and making their life harder.

Conclusion

...

I said at the start of this book that I had four main outcomes I wanted to achieve. Whether I have succeeded or not doesn't feel like my place to say. As with so much of my work, I will leave it up to you to decide.

The one hope I do have is that despite the colourful descriptions, subject matter and punchy title, I really want this book to be viewed as a motivational read, rather than leaving you feeling like we are all doomed.

I have written this book from a place of enormous privilege; namely, I am someone who has always enjoyed my job. Don't get me wrong, there have been some incredibly tough moments – days where the absolutely last thing I wanted to do was drag myself into work – but overall, I have enjoyed the vast majority of it, and I am aware that not everyone is able to say the same.

Getting people to like their job or career more is such a worthwhile goal. Even just the smallest uptick in the number of people happy with their job would have huge benefits. From the mental health of those involved, their sense of fulfilment, to the wider goals of economics and productivity, we all win.

One of the biggest factors that impacts that outcome is defined by your boss. In a lot of ways, it is the only factor. A good boss can make even the worst job enjoyable, and a terrible boss can turn your dream career into a living nightmare.

The more people you get enjoying their jobs, the more productive and motivated they will be. This will in turn help businesses to increase productivity and revenue.

And so the final message I have for you is this: be selfish with your career and do not let these morons dictate whether you get to enjoy your career or not.

Making that first step towards change can feel like the hardest thing in the world and I do not underestimate how much courage it can take to do it. I have, however, never, ever, seen anyone regret leaving a boss who makes them miserable, and sometimes even just beginning the process can feel like the weight of the world has been lifted off your shoulders.

Whether it is quitting or using some of the advice in this book to help make the existing situation better, we spend too much of our time at work not to do everything we can to try and enjoy it.

Life is too short not to.

SOURCES

INTRODUCTION

Perceptyx, 'Nearly A Quarter Of All Employees Are Working For Their Worst Manager', 2023 <https://blog.perceptyx.com/nearly-a-quarter-of-all-employees-are-working-for-the-worst-manager-theyve-ever-had> [accessed 22 April 2025]

CHAPTER 2

Career Arc, 'The State of the Candidate Experience', 2016 <https://d31kswug2i6wp2.cloudfront.net/marketo/content/careerarc-2016-candidate-experience-study.pdf> [accessed 22 April 2025]

Career Plug, '2021 Candidate Experience Report', 2021 <https://www.careerplug.com/wp-content/uploads/2021/09/2021-Candidate-Experience-Report.pdf> [accessed 22 April 2025]

CHAPTER 3

DDI, 'The Frontline Leader Project', 2019 <https://www.ddiworld.com/contact-us/1484/0b0c8fe3-f0ad-45bf-a8e5-49636b4b1434> [accessed 22 April 2025]

Deloitte, 'Core Beliefs and Culture: Chairman's Survey Findings', 2013 <https://www2.deloitte.com/content/dam/Deloitte/global/Documents/About-Deloitte/gx-core-beliefs-and-culture.pdf> [accessed 22 April 2025]

Menasce Horowitz, J., and Parker, K., 'How Americans View Their Jobs', Pew Research Center, March 2023

Oak Engage, 'Toxic Workplace Report 2023', 2023 <https://oak.com/media/v1wp24tf/toxic-workplace-report-final-cleaned.pdf> [accessed 22 April 2025]

TeamStage, 'Productivity Statistics: Key Elements in 2024', 2024 <https://teamstage.io/productivity-statistics/> [accessed 22 April 2025]

CHAPTER 5

Allas, T. and Schaninger, B., 'The Boss Factor: Making the World a Better Place through Workplace Relationships', *McKinsey Quarterly*, September 2020 <https://www.mckinsey.com/capabilities/people-and-organizational-performance/our-insights/the-boss-factor-making-the-world-a-better-place-through-workplace-relationships> [accessed 22 April 2025]

UKG, 'Managers Impact Our Mental Health More Than Doctors, Therapists—and Same as Spouses', February 2023 <https://www.ukg.co.uk/about-us/newsroom/workforce-institute-managers-impact-mental-health> [accessed 22 April 2025]

CHAPTER 7

Perna, M., 'Why Gen Z Is Thriving In The Entrepreneur Life', *Forbes*, June 2024 <https://www.forbes.com/sites/markcperna/2024/06/18/gen-z-thriving-entrepreneurship/> [accessed 23 April 2025]

Walters, R., 'Conscious Unbossing - 52% of Gen-Z Professionals Don't Want to Be Middle Managers', September 2024 <https://www.robertwalters.co.uk/insights/news/blog/conscious-unbossing.html> [accessed 23 April 2025]

CHAPTER 9

Cendon Garcia, D., 'Over 60% of Gen Z Europeans Plan to Start Businesses within the next 3-5 Years, Survey Finds', *EU-Startups*, November 2024 <https://www.eu-startups.com/2024/11/over-60-of-gen-z-europeans-plan-to-start-businesses-within-the-next-3-5-years-survey-finds/> [accessed 23 April 2025]

Hays, 'Work-Life Balance on an Upward Spiral and Different Working Hours Would Improve This Further', September 2023 <https://www.hays.co.uk/media-centre/press-releases/content/work-life-balance-on-upward-spiral> [accessed 23 April 2025]

Weston, T., 'Economic Growth, Inflation and Productivity', House of Lords Library, June 2023 <https://lordslibrary.parliament.uk/economic-growth-inflation-and-productivity/> [accessed 23 April 2025]